E. R.

d. d. d. J. H. Whitfield,

28. v. 49.

DANTE
AND
VIRGIL

BY
J. H. WHITFIELD

BASIL BLACKWELL OXFORD

First published, 1949

Printed in Great Britain for BASIL BLACKWELL & MOTT, LIMITED
by A. R. MOWBRAY & CO. LIMITED, LONDON AND OXFORD

PREFACE

HAD I not been struck by a chance and jocular remark of an old author, *That a Man had as good go to Court without a Cravat, as appear in Print without a Preface*, these few preliminary words might have been left unwritten. For the range and intention of this small book will, I think, be clear. It approaches Dante by way of our connection with him in the English language, and by some attempt to maintain life in that connection; and it proceeds to a survey of his poem which is intelligible to those who are not already acquainted with the *Comedy*, or even with Italian. Then, on the basis of that survey, it continues with an examination of the poetry of Dante in its relation with that of Dante's guide. These two, Dante and Virgil, by virtue of that close association in the *Comedy* as guide and pilgrim, are often taken for granted as being poetically akin. Why else should Dante take Virgil as his master, than because he was like him, or wished to be? And that is something which has prevented men's questionings upon this point. But in reality they stand on different ground, and look in opposite directions. Neither of them is the poet of the modern age, if indeed this latter with its altered outlooks can adopt as its own any poet of the past. But to see sharply and fully the limits, and the contrasts, of their achievements and ideals seems to me an exercise that is not without its relevance for our contemporary world.

September, 1948

CONTENTS

DANTE AND VIRGIL

DANTE FOR THE ENGLISH

IT might be time now to write a history of translations from the Italian, and from the Italians. I shall only be concerned cursorily with this by way of introduction, but if it were written it would bring for attention much in our heritage that we are accustomed to forget, and it would reveal, I think, a pattern of some interest. The ways of travel between two countries, and two cultures, may start by being two: the going there, or the coming here. They gain in complexity when contacts last through nearly six hundred years. We may not only ask ourselves where we shall put up to-day, whether with Pirandello or with Silone, with Papini or D'Annunzio, or what Italian literature is in itself; we must look back as well to see what contribution there has been from the one culture to the other, and by what alchemy it has been transferred from the possession of one nation to the other. Perhaps *transference* is the wrong term to use, for culture partakes of the nature of spiritual goods as defined by Dante, and we may call to mind that passage in *Purgatorio* where Dante feigns surprise that sharing can multiply, and not divide, possession: ' "But if instead love for the highest sphere twisted your desires aloft, this fear would not be in your breast. For all the more who say there, This is ours, each one possesses so much more of good, and burns the more with charity in that sphere." '

> "ché per quanti si dice piú lí—nostro—,
> tanto possiede piú di ben ciascuno,
> e piú di caritate arde in quel chiostro—"

do we not need that charity of mutual possession of cultural things in the Europe of the present? And we may find that the excursion back in search of those elements which we as Englishmen have appropriated from the Italian stock is helpful also in refocusing what is valuable for both England and Italy. We do not live in a world which is stable, or certain of its track. No nation is sure in the possession of its past culture, except in so far as the individuals who compose it seize hold upon that culture to give it life. And no individual is heir to more of the past than what he values. All the more, if we are uncertain of our path, should we look back to discover what is valuable and permanent in what we have, or what we had.

Take up a prospectus of Italian book-production now, and you will see that everything, from Walter Savage Landor down to D. H. Lawrence, or back to Shakespeare, has been or is being translated. It is the reverse of a situation which we once knew. For time was when we in England could afford the importation of most of Italian literature, and of much also that was less than literature, by way of translation. It was not only that the process cost us nothing, except the effort, as there were then no authors' rights. It was a matter, as it is now, of prestige. We took all there was because the sun shone in our eyes. That was the golden age for translation from the Italian: in numbers, and in quality. The English language was fresh from its native soil, rich, but crisp and unworn: how much of the charm of Chaucer lies in the naïvety of his idiom? And here to supplement native invention there was afforded a whole range of works that had attained maturity. Sometimes the process of appropriation botched what was delicate, and not only in the beginning when men were groping for the sense, or for the flow of words. Who would not find Wyatt clumsier than Petrarch? or who could think Spenser superior to Ariosto, or to Tasso? But in this work of penetration it was not impossible for the Italian original to gain something in its passage into virgin soil. Read Ronsard imitating a neo-Latin poet like Marullus, and you will find something that was smooth and just a little tired reviving as it passes into a younger idiom. So it was when some, at least, of the works of the later Italian Renascence passed into English. Read Fairfax, he will not only hold his own with the Tasso of the epic, you may find as well that Fairfax has qualities which Tasso lacked, and that the *Gerusalemme Liberata*, in becoming *Godfrey of Bulloigne*, has added to its spirit something that one is glad to have acquired. Tasso is noble, but just a little general and imprecise: Fairfax gives to him a concreteness, and a raciness that is all his own. This is a matter to which I can return in the assessment of Tasso's quality as poet, and here I can content myself with the indications which are necessary to show a method of translation. Thus Tasso wrote:

> Ne sorride il superbo, e gli risponde:
> Che fa dunque Tancredi, e dove stassi?   (VII, 85)

The corners of the lines are filled with pronouns, which seem legitimate, but have no energy; and the second half of the question is only a variant of the first. It supports the dignity of the line, but it does not press home any point about Tancred's non-appearance. Now look at Fairfax making the situation clear:

> The *Pagan* cast a scornful smile and said
> But where is *Tancred*, is he still in Bed?

The vagueness of the pronouns has gone out, and a concrete symbol of the accusation against Tancred (that of cowardice) has entered in their room. I give one other comparison, and at a point which the reader will recognize. Tasso is often neo-Virgilian—it was his right, and he manages it with dignity, though with just a little unoriginality in one who is not translating. I take him, perhaps, at his most successful:

> Era la notte allor ch'alto riposo
> Han l'onde e i venti, e parea muto il mondo;
> Gli animai lassi, e quei che'l mare ondoso,
> O de'liquidi laghi alberga il fondo,
> E chi si giace in tana, o in mandra ascoso,
> E i pinti augelli nell'oblio profondo
> Sotto il silenzio de'secreti orrori
> Sopian gli affanni, e raddolciano i cori.   (II, 96)

It is not untypical of Tasso that the details here are vague, or lacking, while the one word with most relief stands out as Virgil's rather than Tasso's contribution—*pictaeque volucres*. For the rest, the effect is blurred by spreading statement and repetitions. If the waves are stilled what use, other than a conventional one, is left for the *ondoso*? are not lakes liquid usually? and if the fishes of the sea and the lakes are separately asleep, then why not those as well of the rivers and the streams? And how much do the last two lines add to the sense, or the effect, of the strong line which precedes them? It is because of things like these that Fairfax,

when he was translating Tasso, constantly found the chance of
saying other, and more, than his original:

> Now spread the Night her spangled Canopy,
> And summon'd every restless Eye to Sleep:
> On Beds of tender Grass the Beasts down ly,
> The Fishes slumbred in the silent Deep,
> Unheard was Serpents Hiss, and Dragons Cry,
> Birds left to sing, and *Philomen* to weep,
>   Only that Noise Heav'ns rolling Circles kest,
>   Sung Lullaby to bring the world to Rest.

What Tasso said has shrunk, in Fairfax's hands, to its essential
statement; and the space left at his disposal he is poet enough to
use for his own purposes.

Now that is one method of translating. It was that of Fairfax,
and of some others of his time. We may find it again in the
translator who is Fairfax's most worthy successor, in Sir Richard
Fanshawe. The *Pastor Fido* was less than the *Gerusalemme*, more
languid, more diffuse. Fanshawe, in bringing to its translation
into English an ability as great as that of Fairfax, wrought a
greater miracle, and left behind him to be forgotten (or even
to be passed over for his *Lusiads*, his dullest work) *The Faithfull
Shepherd*, one of the most attractive of the unread poems in a
century which is often combed for interest. And prefixed to his
version there are some lines of Sir John Denham on the subject
of translators and translations which may assist our judgment.
They begin with a condemnation, but perhaps the condemnation
was not needed then, and we might store it for a later period,

> Such is our Pride, our Folly, or our Fate,
> That few but such as cannot write, translate.

There will be other ages, will there not? when such a warning
might have had its use. In the meantime, it is the praise for
Fanshawe which gives the recipe for seventeenth-century translation, once it had passed that earlier stage of striving to make out
a sense but dimly understood:

> That servile Path thou nobly dost decline
> Of tracing word by word, and line by line.
> Those are the labour'd births of slavish brains,
> Not the effects of Poetry, but Pains.

Cheap vulgar arts, whose narrownesse affords
No flight for thoughts, but poorly sticks at words.
A new and nobler way thou dost pursue
To make Translations and Translators too.
They but preserve the Ashes, Thou the Flame,
True to his sense, but truer to his fame.

Or perhaps even we might amend the formula: for Fairfax and
Fanshawe both are capable of kindling a flame, a brightness,
where the original in its smoothness fell rather short of that.
It is not my business to quote much from Guarini, though he is
very quotable, and Fanshawe more so, and though much remains
to say upon Guarini's influence, as Ben Jonson indicated:

> All our English writers,
> I mean such as are happy in the Italian,
> Will deign to steal out of this author, mainly:
> Almost as much as from Montagnié:
> He has so modern and facile a vein,
> Fitting the time, and catching the court-ear![1]

But let us take the *Pastor Fido* at one point where the facile vein of
Guarini caught the ear of Molière as well as Fanshawe, and where,
with the lightest of touches, we may see the English poet giving
a freshness which is new:

> O Primavera, gioventú dell'anno,
> Bella madre di fiori,
> D'erbe novelle e di novelli amori;
> Tu torni ben, ma teco
> Non tornano i sereni
> E fortunati dí delle mie gioie:
> Tu torni ben, tu torni;
> Ma teco altro non torna,
> Che del perduto mio caro tesoro
> La rimembranza misera e dolente.   (III, i)

Who could say that this lament of Mirtillo is unsuccessful?
It is only if we turn to a sonnet of Petrarch's, *Zefiro torna e'l bel
tempo rimena*, that we may realize that this is too practised, too
rehearsed, and that in the process it has lost vitality. But in the
meantime, is it not more successful than Molière's imitation of it?

> Arbres épais, et vous, prés émaillés,
> La beauté dont l'hiver vous avoit depouillés
> Par le printemps vous est rendue;

[1] *Volpone* III, ii.

Vous reprenez tous vos appas:
Mais mon âme ne reprend pas
La joie, hélas ! que j'ai perdue.[1]

Guarini lingers over the theme with practised repetitions, while
Molière dismisses it; but Fanshawe rejuvenates it all:

Spring, the yeers youth, fair Mother of new flowrs,
New leaves, new loves, drawn by the winged hours,
Thou art return'd; but the felicity
Thou brought'st me last is not return'd with thee.
Thou art return'd, but nought returns with thee
Save my lost joyes regretfull memory.

The steps aside, the *petits pas* which modify the tone of the
original, are slighter there than those taken by Fairfax; but they
are not for that reason less effective in kindling an enthusiasm
which escapes the polish of Guarini's idiom. And Fanshawe is no
less delightful an experience than Fairfax: someone who wrote
when the solemnity of Milton was in the air, and was untouched
by it.

But am I not to be reproached? It was with Dante and his
Englishing that I was to be concerned, and so far at least it is other
names that I have put forward. But even so, I have been still
concerned, though indirectly, with this matter of Dante. What
have I said, but that there was a time when the English knew
how to write, and profited by a general admiration for Italian
literature to transplant it all? And what have I to add, except that
when we knew by native wit how to write well, we did not, by a
miscalculation, count Dante in amongst that all? Chaucer had
heard of Dante's fame—for he was near enough—but in the
golden age of translations into English, Dante's reputation was
in eclipse. Lady Politick Would-be, in the same passage of
Volpone which attests the popularity of *Pastor Fido*, added a line
later what was perhaps an understatement:

Dante is hard, and few can understand him.

In conformity with this pronouncement—more honest, one may
be sure, than her claim before to have read Dante[2]—there is no

---

[1] *Princesse d'Elide*, Troisième Intermède, sc. ii.
[2] *Volpone, ibid.* Which of your poets? Petrarch, or Tasso, or Dante?
Guarini? Ariosto? Aretine?
Cieco di Hadria? I have read them all.
It is an instructive list, not least in its order.

household Elizabethan name, as Hoby, Harington, or Fairfax himself, attached to Dante. Maybe we are the poorer because of that: but maybe also that the *Divine Comedy* was not in need, like the *Pastor Fido*, of rejuvenation; that it would not have lent itself agreeably to being shrunk by a Fairfax to be filled out again to a new outline; and that the formula of Denham was not admissible for tackling anything as precise as Dante's poetry.

Before we come to another formula than this, and to Dante himself translated, there is an interlude. Fanshawe, whose *Faithfull Shepherd* dates from 1647, marks the end, I think, of the old series of the verse translators. He was the cavalier (was he not married at Oxford during the siege, and at Wolvercot Church?) who dealt cavalierly, with the spirit and the touch of a gentleman, but without any 'poetic' diction. His work held men's interest for a century, but in the meantime the accent is shifting away from poetry. After all, were we not advancing to sedate and sober middle age?

> A *Vertuoso* was taken yesterday by the Marshals belonging to the Court of the Censors of Learning, who was found with his Spectacles on his Nose, reading some Italian Poetrie; and this morning early, by order from *Apollo*, he received three sound lashes with a cord first, and was afterwards told, that being, as he was, *of the age of 55 years, he should learn to apply himself to graver studies, and leave the reading of those Madrigals, Songs, and Sonnets, to be idlely spent by those spruce Youngsters, in whom those things were tolerated, which were severely punished in old men.*

Is not the wind changing? This is the VIIth Advertisement from Parnassus, put into English by Henry Cary, Earl of Monmouth, in 1656; and so much was Boccalini's humour to our liking that this version was reprinted in 1669 and 1674 before another translator took a turn, adapting the *Ragguagli* 'to the present times' in 1704. And if Boccalini is not himself quite a grave author, there are others, like Father Paul, or Machiavelli (the editions of the *Works* succeeding in a long series to the translations of separate works, and to the misrepresentations of Gentillet) to keep him numerous company. These uncharted seas are not without their interest, nor their importance for the seventeenth-century mind[1]: wit, politics, divinity and history was what we wanted mainly to import in the second half of the seventeenth century. We had

---

[1] Not quite uncharted, see Z. S. Fink, *The Classical Republicans*, 1945.

left Italian Poetrie for Italian prose. This already was a narrowing
of the attention we had given to Italy. The eighteenth century
followed, and our interest shifted resolutely from the Italian
to the classical world. Does not Addison point the way from the
beginning of that century? The epigraphs to his *Spectators* are
from Horace or Juvenal, Virgil or Cicero, and though he may
quote exceptionally Boccalini as 'that judicious author,'[1] yet
Tasso, to confirm the veering of the wind, is only on the edge of
Addison's discussion of Milton's value as a poet, nor does he figure
very well. 'I might have also inserted several passages in Tasso,
which our Author has imitated; but as I do not look upon Tasso
to be a sufficient voucher, I would not perplex my reader with
such quotations as might do more honour to the Italian than the
English poet.'[2] It is a pious, and a contemptuous, exclusion.
And the same Addison, as he travels in Italy, looks for the Latin
poets and their scenery. His is not the method of the Président de
Brosses, the epitome of taste in the first half of the eighteenth
century: nor that of Lady Morgan with her view of society at the
beginning of the nineteenth. He quotes Lucan or Virgil at every
turn where the landscape lets him, and if he rarely adds a modern
Italian, it will be only one who chose to write in elegant Latin,
as Sannazaro in his elegies, or in *De Partu Virginis*. And similarly,
it is these Italians of the Renascence who had written in Latin who
are game now for the editor and translator. Pope praises Vida,

> Immortal Vida, on whose honour'd Brow,
> The Poet's Bays and Criticks' Ivy grow;
> Cremona now shall ever boast thy Name,
> As next in Place to Mantua, next in Fame,

and reprints as well to point his praise the anthology of neo-Latin
poetry; and round him the English with an itch to versify versify
Vida's *Art of Poetry*, his *Game of Chess*, even his *Christiad*. Nor in
this exercise was the Rev. Christopher Pitt more than one in a
regiment, and the fortunes of Vida, as a symbol of our Latin interests in the eighteenth century, are a portent. True, when all was
said and done, there emerged (rather than remained as a constant)
a salvage from our Italian interests: it was our patronage for the
epic poets. Does not Gibbon sum it up with his epithet, 'the
incomparable Ariosto,' as Charles James Fox with his enthusiasm?

---

[1] *Spectator*, No. 291.   [2] *ibid.*, No. 369.

And thus it is that later on, over a century after Fanshawe, and when the flood of classicism has let poetic diction grow and thicken, Tasso and Ariosto were made to speak a new and more tedious language. It is an odd thing that the supporters of Latin as an educational discipline have always insisted that it taught as nothing else could, how one should write English; and that the neo-classical ages have been for us unfortunate in style. Indeed, though, I remember from one of those school editions of one book of Virgil's *Aeneid* a reverend editor who made the largest claims for Latin as the schoolmaster of pure English. Occasionally in his notes, he showed the way it should be wrote, and one of his jewels sticks still in my mind. It is Hecuba addressing Priam when he was distraught: 'What dire resolve drove thee to gird yon arms?' It is as good, if you are so minded, as the *mobled queen*; and if you are not so minded it is as deadening as John Hoole. And if before we hesitated, this time we can be sure: it is a mercy that the reputation of Dante has not been reborn for him to stand, in Hoole's translation, alongside his other victims. But while we may be grateful for that mercy, we must not forget that the dull Hoole, when he transmuted the gold of Ariosto and of Tasso to his own private lead,[1] established with the tedious amplification of the dead eighteenth-century poetic idiom a model for poetic translations after him.

There is no need for me to remind the reader of that rebirth of interest in Dante at the end of the eighteenth century. From being out of the ranking, he is to become *hors pair*. Petrarch and Tasso, who had shared the homages of Europe as the supreme Italian poet, lose caste, and ground; and Dante steps up to share with Shakespeare the tributes of the modern age. Once Carlyle had established the apotheosis of Dante, the Poet as Hero, and Lord Vernon shown the way to Dante criticism, nineteenth-century England set to work with zeal. We are not here concerned with the fruits of scholarship, and I can return later to the work of the Moores and the Paget Toynbees, though meanwhile we have the right to pride in the contribution which they made to Dante-knowledge. But the reader may well be afraid that I shall be concerned with the spate of translations which, even from the Rev. Henry Boyd in 1785, began to make amends for centuries of neglect. For now the situation was almost in reverse

---

[1] *Comment en un plomb vil l'or pur s'est-il changé?*

B

of what we saw at first; it was Dante without the rest who took
our eye, and perhaps the bulk of English translation and illustration of Dante in the nineteenth century might come near to
equalling all the translations of the Elizabethan age. I must con-
fess, though, I am no professional reader of translations into
English, unless they were made before the days of Dyer and of
Hoole. In these matters I am a coward, like Falstaff, upon instinct.
It is on instinct that I feel the legacy of Hoole clings round the
nineteenth-century attempts at translation. The desire for a
respectable rotundity spreads far. There is at the beginning of the
Dies Irae a stark and solemn verse,

> Tuba mirum spargens sonum
> Per sepulchra regionum
> Coget omnes ante thronum.

You see how bare it is as idiom, and how imposing. Now listen
to it in nineteenth-century English:

> Hark! the trumpet sounds appalling,
> Earth's sepultured dead up-calling,
> Prostrate round the Lord's throne falling!

You see how opposite a procedure this is to the one we found
before: Fairfax concentrated Tasso, then filled the stanza with
his own novelty; but here the sense of the original expands on
contact with the English language as if by some hidden, but
uniform, law of nature. It is like, is it not, the frog's egg, round
whose black speck a coat of jelly swells when it makes contact
with the water. And with this formula of amplification there is
no room for the old sprightliness and freshness. It is not only
the equivocation of that piteous *appalling* that makes those lines
bathetic, it is the effort after diction at the very moment of dis-
persing it. Writing consists, perhaps, either in unwrapping, or in
wrapping up; but it all depends on what you unwrap, and on
who does the wrapping up. Nor was Dante, who can be as
immediate in his statements as the author of the *Dies Irae* a good
subject for the nineteenth century to practise on. Once more,
I do not wish to claim extensive acquaintance with the set of
translations from Dante which we have inherited, nor is there
any need for them to sink always to the bathos of those lines
which I have quoted from the *Dies Irae*, but I think if we were to
look from Dante himself to an anthology of translated passages

like that edited by Paget Toynbee with the title *In the Footsteps of Dante* we should end with the impression that the footsteps lead away, and not behind. If I may put it modestly, so as to secure agreement with the formula, I should say that, in spite of the English nineteenth-century interest in Dante, Dante is very unlike, poetically, the English nineteenth century.

Have we not here a proof to hand? Which of us now (and I am not speaking of those who accept the prose of the Temple Classics edition as a prop they need), which of us now comes to read Dante via that English interpretation of him in the last century? And how many go on from Dante to the Boyds, the Carys, the Plumptres, or the Warren Vernons? Dante was as much our poet as Shakespeare was the Germans', and we hedged him round with more than as much apparatus. But that fervour ended, we may fairly say, where the nineteenth century ends itself, with the coming of war in 1914. After that, in spite of the centenary of 1921, Dante had ceased to command as large an English audience as formerly. The tradition of Dante scholarship had a few survivors, but no true successors; and with the failure of that tradition, the apparatus of a century lay neglected in the libraries and in the bookshops. What was saved was exported into the commentaries; but much of the rest was rust that clings to the form that the strength has left, hard and curled and ready to snap. Can we not see it in the surviving English edition of the text of Dante, with its dated scholarship, its stilted and unnatural translation? It belongs still to the world of the nineteenth century, and we might find that it brings a dwindling company of readers to Dante's poem. Even the authority of Mr. Eliot, who inherited his view of Dante from the English nineteenth century, while being at the same time wise enough to throw their method all away, was not enough, perhaps, to restore Dante to the place he used to hold, or to do this more than nominally; so that we run the risk of having Dante placed, like Voltaire's Homer, on an exalted, and unexamined, pedestal. *C'est un fort grand auteur: personne ne le lit.* That is something of which we should take stock, for the traditional valuation of Dante rests on the work of men whom we have thrown away. Their ranking may be right, their comprehension may be wrong: in any case we shall do well to start afresh, not with the spirit of iconoclasm, but with the hope of making a contact that has been choked.

Certainly we cannot do so by reverting to the methods of Edward Moore or Paget Toynbee, as against that of Mr. Eliot; and I have thought that we might find a preliminary clue in the latter's essay on Dante. The reader will remember his discussion of the difference between Dante and Shakespeare in poetic technique, his contrast between the complicated metaphor of Shakespeare

(Put up your bright swords, lest the dew rust them),

and the simplicity of such a line as

"E'n la sua volontade è nostra pace."

Faced with this difference Mr. Eliot expressed the conviction that Dante should lose less in translation into English, than would Shakespeare going into Italian. That is, I think, true, even if every line of Dante is not so straightforward as this sample; but it is only true if we break with all the accretions and amplifications which the old translator's-jargon had imposed on us. Have we not now the scruples of scholarship to keep us both from this, and (even if we inherited the talent, and the spirit), from the licence of Fairfax or Fanshawe? There is one solution which I think in Dante's case is possible: to see how much can be done with a prose which need have no commitments to the building up of a new verse façade, and which can therefore be something other than one extra in the long, and by now inefficacious, series of the verse translations. It must not be a prose which abjures poetry, or turns the *Divine Comedy* into a novel; nor need it be. Indeed, if Mr. Eliot was right in his statement on the nature of Dante's poetry, there is every reason to suppose that to follow Dante in this way, without forcing an effect, but without renouncing those that come, may be nearer to him than what has been achieved. And it is a pity that Mr. Eliot did not himself exploit the possibilities in the explanatory translations which he appended to his own quotations from Dante's text. Such a translation will halt between prose and poetry. That is not wrong, or even inconvenient, since it seems to me the first duty of scholarship to provide new impetus for turning to Dante's text, and for the understanding of Dante's quality and his position not through old clouds, but through a fresh approach. It is in this spirit, and with in mind the lessened hold of Dante in England as compared with fifty years ago, that I have begun this volume with a tentative translation of the beginning of Dante's poem. For such a beginning has two utilities: it may lead outwards, to a knowledge of Dante's text; and it may lead inwards also, to the account of Dante's poem which follows it, and so to the comparison which I have attempted between Dante and his master, Virgil. The opening passages of the *Inferno*, down to the episode of Paolo and Francesca, are, if we suspend inquiry for a moment into the system of Dante's ideas in Canto I, graphic and self-explanatory. In translating them I have shunned the use of words which are archaic, or which are thought in themselves to have a poetic rank: a troublesome company, and more rank than odorous. It is not only we who have been clogged with them, and it is wise to remember that the Italian for the Unknown Soldier is not Soldato Sconosciuto, but Milite Ignoto. But such usage is not that of Dante, and is, I venture to think, as well inimical to the establishment of anything that is of worth as poetry. I pass, then, to the opening of Dante's poem.

DANTE'S HELL

IN the middle of the passage of our life I found myself in a dark wood, for the straight path was lost. How hard it is to say what this wood was, wild and rough and strong, renewing fear when I think of it! So bitter was it that death itself is little more. But so that I may come to the good I found there I will speak first of the other things I saw. I cannot say well how I came to it, so full I was of sleep just at that point when I abandoned the true way. But when I had arrived at a hill's foot, there where the valley ended which had pierced my heart with fear, I looked aloft, and saw the shoulders of the hill. They were clothed already with the rays of the planet that leads men straight by every path. Then was the fear a little stilled which had remained in my heart's lake all through the night I passed in such distress, and as a man who with a panting breath comes from the ocean to the shore, turns back and looks upon the perilous wave, so did my mind, still bent on flight, look back to see that pass which no man ever left alive. Then when my weary body had a little rest, I took my way again on the deserted slope so that the firm foot always was below. And lo, almost at the beginning of the steep, a panther, very light and quick, covered with spotted coat, would not depart out of my way, but rather hindered it so much that many times I turned in order to return. It was the opening of the day. The sun was mounting up with those same stars that were with him when the divine love first moved those lovely things: so that the hour and the sweet season was a cause for hoping well about the beast with spotted skin. That hope was not enough to stop the fear I felt at the appearance of a lion. He seemed to come against me with high head and hungry rage, so that the air seemed fearful of his roar. And a she-wolf, whose meagre frame seemed burdened with the sum of all desire, and many had she made to live in wretchedness, weighed so upon me with the fear her sight gave to me, that I lost the hope of climbing to the height. Just as the man who gathers in with zest, and the time comes for him to lose, so that in all his thoughts he weeps and is distressed, so was for me this peaceless beast which, coming on me, drove me slowly back where no sun shines. Then while I tumbled to this lowly place, one who seemed weak through lengthy silence was offered to my gaze. And when I saw him in this desert, 'Have mercy on me,' shouted I to him, 'whoever you may be, whether shade or very man!' He answered me: 'No man, a man I was, my parents were of Lombardy, both born in Mantua. My birth was under Julius, though it was late. I lived in Rome under the good Augustus, in the time of false and lying gods. I was a poet, and I sang of that just son Anchises had who came from Troy after proud Ilium was burnt. But why do you go back to so much pain? Why do you not climb the pleasant hill which is the fount and cause of every joy?' 'O, are you then that Virgil and that spring which spreads so broad a stream of song?' I answered him with lowly brow. 'Honour and light of every poet, may the long zeal and the great love that made me seek your volume out stand in my stead. You are my master and my author; you alone are he from whom I took the style has brought me honour. You see the beast that made me turn: help me from her, o famous sage, for she has made me tremble in my veins and pulse.' 'It is another journey you must take,' he answered when he saw me weep, 'if you wish safety from this savage place. This beast that makes you cry for help lets no one pass upon her way, but stops them so that in the end she kills. Her nature is so cruel and so bad that never can she fill her longing lust, but after eating has more hunger than before. Many are those animals with which she weds, and more shall be, before there comes the Hound to put her to her death with pain. This Hound shall feed on neither land nor wealth, only on wisdom, virtue, love; his birth shall be between Feltro and Feltro. He shall be saviour of that low Italy for which there died the maid Camilla, Euryalus, Turnus and Nisus of their wounds; and he shall drive her out of every town until he sends her back to hell whence the first envy brought her. So for your good I think that you must follow me, and I will be your guide; and I will take you hence through an eternal place, where you shall hear despairing shrieks, where you shall see the ancient spirits, each of whom cries out of second death. And you shall see those that are happy in the fire because they hope to come, whenever it may be, among the blessed; and if you will go up among these last, one there shall be worthier for that than me. With her at my departure I will leave you; for that emperor who reigns up there, since I was rebel to his law, lets me not come into his city. In all parts he holds sway and there he reigns; there is his city and his throne; how happy is the man who is elect!' And I to him: 'Poet, I beg of you for that God's sake you did not know, so that I flee this danger and a worse, that you will take me where you just have said. Bring me to see St. Peter's gate, and those whom you make out to be so sad.' Then he moved off, and I went after him.

CANTO II

The day was dying, and the darkening air took from their labours all the creatures that there are on earth; and I alone prepared to undergo the strife both of the way, and of the pity, which faithful memory shall set down. O Muses, o lofty mind, now give me help. O memory that wrote down all I saw, now shall appear your nobleness. I began: 'Poet, and guide, look to my worth, if I am good enough, ere you commit me to this enterprise. You say that Silvius's father, in mortal body still, went into the immortal world, and with his senses knew it. But if the enemy of all ill things was liberal to him thus, he does not seem unworthy to an understanding man who thinks what greatness was to come of him, and who and what he was: for he was chosen in the empyrean heaven as father of fair Rome and of the empire, both of which, to tell the truth, had been established for the holy place where the successors of great Peter were to sit. By this journey which you added to his fame he learnt of things that were the cause both of his victory, and of the papal mantle too. There went there then the Chosen Vessel, to bring back comfort for that faith which is beginning of salvation's way. But why should I come there? or who allows it me? I am not Aeneas, nor am I Paul; nor I nor others rate me worthy of it. Therefore, if I say that I will come, I am afraid my coming may be impious. You are wise: you understand me better than I speak.' And as the man who turns from what he wished, changing his mind upon new thoughts, so that he leaves entirely what he had begun, just so was I on that dark slope, for as I thought, I took right to its close this undertaking that had been so quick begun. 'If I have rightly understood your words,' answered the shade of that great-minded man, 'your mind is now beset by cowardice, which often fastens on a man and turns him from some honourable enterprise, like a horse shying at an imagined sight. I will tell you why I came and what I heard, at the first moment when I grieved for you, so that you may be free from this your fear. I was with those held in suspense; and then a lady, blessed and beautiful, called to me, so that I asked for her command. Her eyes shone, more than does the star; and she began to speak to me, soft and low, with angel's voice and in an angel's tongue: "O courteous soul from Mantua, whose fame still lasts up in the world, and will, as long as lasts the world, my friend, not Fortune's friend, is hindered on the desert slope so in his way that he has turned for fear. I am afraid he may already be so lost that I have risen late to bring him help, from what I heard of him in heaven. Now go, and with your noble speech and all he needs for his escape, so help him that I may be consoled. I am Beatrice who send you out; I come whence I desire return. Love sent me forth, and makes me speak. When once again I am before my lord then I will often sing your praise to him." Then was she silent, and then I began: "O lady full of virtue, by whom alone our human race rises above the content of that heaven whose circuit is the least, so much is your command my liking that the obedience, if it were done already, would be slow. There is no need for more than to have opened your desires to me. But tell me why you do not shrink from coming here, down to this centre from the ample place to which you wish return." She answered me, "Since you are anxious to pursue knowledge so far, I will say briefly why I do not fear to come in here. One must fear those things alone which have the power to do men harm, and others not, for in them lies no fear. I, by God's mercy, am so made as to remain untouched by this your misery, nor does a flame from this fire hurt me. There is a gentle lady up in heaven who grieves over this impediment to which I send you, so that harsh judgment there is broken. She asked St. Lucy for her help, and said: 'Your follower now has need of you, and I commend him to your care.' Lucy, the enemy of every cruel one, rose up and came to where I sat with ancient Rachel. She said: 'Beatrice, true praise of God, why do you give no help to him who loved you so, who left the vulgar throng for you? do you not hear the pity of his cry? do you not see death stalk him by the river that is dangerous as the sea?' Never on earth were persons quick to follow profit or to shun their loss as I when I had heard these words. I came down here from my blessed seat, trusting to your noble speech, which honours you and those that hear it too." When she had told me this she weeping turned her shining eyes away, so that she made me faster in my coming; and I came to you even as she turned. I took you from before that beast which cut you off from the short passage of the pleasant hill. Then, what is this? why, why do you stay? why do you nourish so much cowardice at heart? why are you not bold and frank, since in heaven's court are three such blessed ladies to take care of you, and since my words make promise to you of such good?' Just as the flowers, though shut and drooping after frost by night, when the sun lights them rise all open on their stems, so did my drooping spirits rouse, and such good will ran in my heart that I began as one who had no fear: 'O kind was she who succoured me! and courteous are you in giving her such quick obedience to the true words she spoke to you! You have disposed my heart to come with such desire that I am back once more in my first mind. Go then, one wish unites us both: you are the guide, you are the lord, and you the master too.' So said I to him; and when he moved I entered on the deep and woody way.

CANTO III

'Through me one goes into the grieving city, through me one goes into eternal grief, through me one goes among the lost. Justice moved my high maker; divine power made me, supreme wisdom and primal love. Before me were no created things, except eternal ones, and I remain eternally. Leave all your hopes, o you who enter here.' These words I saw written in dark colour up above a gate; and I: 'Master, their sense is hard for me.' And he to me, as one who judges well: 'Here must you leave all doubts behind; all cowardice must die here. We have come here to the place in which I told you you will see those ones who sorrow, having lost the good of the mind.' Then, with smiling face, he put his hand on mine, and I took comfort, and he led me in within the secret things. Here sighs and tears and shrieks of woe resounded in the starless air, so that at first I wept. Strange tongues and horrid speech, words of grief, accents of anger, voices loud or weak, the clap of hands with them, all made a tumult which revolves for ever in that dark and timeless air. And I whose head was girt with horror said: 'Master, what is this I hear? and who are these who seem so overcome with grief?' And he to me: 'The sad souls of those who lived with neither infamy or praise are in this wretched plight, and they are mixed with that poor choir of angels who are neither rebels nor faithful to their God, but were for themselves. The heavens drive them out in order not to be less beautiful, nor does deep hell receive them, for the guilty there would have some glory over them.' And I: 'Master, what weighs upon them so, that they lament so loud?' He answered: 'I will tell you in few words. These have no hope of death, and yet their blind life is so low that they are jealous of all other fates. The world has left no fame of them; mercy and justice scorn them; do not let us speak of them, but look and pass.' And I, who looked, saw a banner running round so fast as seeming to deserve no rest. After it there came so long a trail of followers that I should never have believed death had undone so many. When I had recognized some of them there I saw, and knew, the shade of him who made through cowardice the great refusal. At once I understood, at once was sure, this was the band of wretches hateful both to God and to his enemies. These hapless ones, who never were alive, were naked, troubled much with flies and wasps. These streaked their faces with their blood, and this, mixed with their tears, was gathered up by loath-some worms under their feet. Then when I turned to look beyond I saw people upon the bank of a great river; so I said: 'Master, grant me to know who these are, and what the custom is that makes them seem so anxious to cross over, as I can see by the weak light.' And he said to me: 'These are things which shall be known to you when we set foot by the sad river Acheron.' Then shamefaced with downcast eyes, fearing my words were troublesome to him, I ceased from speaking till we reached the riverbank. And lo, there came by boat towards us an old man, white through hoary hair, crying: 'Woe to you, wicked souls! hope for no sight of heaven here. I come to take you to the other bank, to everlasting shadow, heat and frost. And you there, living soul, depart from these that are already dead.' But when he saw that I did not depart, he said: 'By another way, and other ports, you will come to the shore, not here, to pass: a lighter boat must take you.' My guide to him: 'Charon, be not cross: it is

willed so where what one wishes, that one can. No more have
you to ask.' Then quiet were the shaggy cheeks of the pilot of
the livid marsh, who had wheels of flame about his eyes. But the
souls, tired and naked, changed colour, with chattering teeth,
when they heard the cruel words. They railed on God and on
their parents, on the human race, the place, the time, the seed of
their conception and their birth; then drew themselves together
weeping fast to this bad bank that waits for all who have no fear
of God. The demon Charon, with his ember-eyes, makes sign
to them, and takes them all, beats with his oar whoever lags
behind. As in autumn the leaves fall one by one, until the bough
gives all its mantle to the ground, so there Adam's bad seed each
at his sign jumps from the shore, like hawks called in by lure.
So they go off over the gloomy wave, and sooner than they
land upon the other side, a new throng gathers over here. 'My
son,' my courteous master said, 'those dying in the wrath of God
come here from every land; and they are ready to cross the stream,
for heavenly justice spurs them on, till fear turns to desire. No
good soul ever passes here; and so, if Charon here complains of
you, now you may know what his words mean.' When this
was said, the gloomy countryside trembled so sharp that still I
run with sweat at my remembered fear. The tearful earth gave
forth a wind, a crimson lightning flashed which conquered all my
sense. I fell as falls a man taken with sleep.

CANTO IV

A heavy thunderclap broke my deep sleep within my mind,
so that I started up as one awaked by force. I stood erect, and
cast my rested eye around, looked hard to know the place where I
might be. I found myself upon the edge of the grievous valley
of the pit which holds thunder of infinite woe. Dark it was, and
deep, and shrouded so that though I tried to pierce it with my
sight, I could see nothing there. 'Now let us go down into the
blind world' began the poet turning pale: 'I will go first, you
follow me.' And I, who saw his colour change: 'How shall I
come, when you fear, who are accustomed comfort to my
doubts?' And he to me: 'Anguish for those who are beneath us
here paints on my face the pity which you take for fear. Come,
for the long way urges us.' So he set out, and so he took me in

to the first circle girding the abyss. Here, as far as I could hear, there was no weeping else than sighs that trembled in the ever-lasting air. This came from grief, not punishments, which all these great throngs had, infants, women, men. The good master said to me: 'You do not ask what are these spirits which you see? I wish you now to know before you further go, they did not sin; and yet if they have merit, it is not enough, since they lacked baptism, the gateway to the faith which you believe. And if they were before the Christian age, they did not rightly worship God: and of these same am I myself. For such defects, and for no other sin, we here are lost, and only in so much offended that without hope we live on in desire.' Great grief seized on my heart when I heard this, because I knew that people of much worth were in limbo in suspense. 'Tell me, master, tell me, lord,' began I in desire to be made sure about that faith which conquers error: 'Did ever anyone come out, for his own merits or through another's, to be blessed?' And he, who understood my covert speech, replied: 'New was I in this state when here I saw arrive a powerful One, crowned with the sign of victory. He drew from hence the shade of the first father, of his son Abel, and of Noah; of the law-giver Moses, the obedient; Abraham the patriarch, David the king; Israel with his father and his sons, and Rachel too, for whom he served so long; and many more, and made them blessed; and I would have you know that, before these, there were no human spirits that were saved.' We did not leave our going for his speech, but passed still on across the wood, the wood, I mean, of thronging souls. Our way was still not long after my sleep before I saw a fire that overcame a hemisphere of darkness. We were as yet some little off it, yet not so much but that I saw in part that people to be honoured held this place. 'O you who honour knowledge and art, who are these so honoured that they are parted from the other souls?' And he to me: 'The honoured name they bear up in your life wins favour for them out of heaven to advance them so.' Meanwhile I heard a voice say: 'Honour the most high poet: his shade had left us, and it now returns.' Then when that voice was still, I saw four great shades come towards us, and their looks were neither sad nor gay. The good master said to me: 'Look at this one with sword in hand, who comes as lord before the other three. This is Homer, sovereign poet; the next is Horace, who wrote the satires; the third is Ovid, and Lucan is the last. Since each bears equally with me the name the one voice spoke alone, they do me honour, and in that do well.' So did I see together met the school of that master of the highest song, who soars like eagle over all the rest. When they had talked amongst themselves somewhat, they turned to me with beckoned greetings, whereat my master smiled. And much more honour did they do to me, making me one of their own throng, so that I was the sixth amongst such wisdom. Thus did we go as far as to the light, speaking of things which it is well to leave unspoken here. We came before a noble castle, seven times encircled with high walls, defended round by a fine stream. This we passed over like dry ground; through seven doors I entered with these seers, and then we came onto a lawn all cool and green. Here there were men with slow grave eyes, full of authority in their appearance. Little they spoke, but with sweet voice. We went a little on one side, into an open place, lighted and high, so that they all could thus be seen. There, facing me, upon the green enamel of the lawn, were shown me the great spirits, such as I exult at having seen. I saw Electra, and many with her, among whom I knew Hector and Aeneas, Caesar armed, with hawk-like eyes. I saw Camilla and Penthesilea on the other side; I saw the king Latinus sitting there, Lavinia his daughter with him. I saw that Brutus who drove Tarquin out, Lucrece, Julia, Martia and Cornelia; and standing by himself upon one side I saw the Saladin. Then when I raised my eyes somewhat, I saw the master of all those who know, sitting among his philosophic heirs. All look to him, all honour him. Here did I see Plato and Socrates, who more than all the rest stand close to him; Democritus, who rates the world as chance, Diogenes, Anaxagoras and Thales, Empedocles, Heraclitus and Zeno; I saw the good collector of the qualities, I mean Dioscorides; Orpheus I saw, Tully and Linus and Seneca the moralist; Euclid, inventor of geometry, and Ptolemy, Hippocrates, Avicenna, Galen; Averroes, who wrote the commentary. I cannot tell fully of all, for the long tally drives me on so much that oftentimes my words must fail my theme. The company of six now loses two: and my wise guide takes me another way, out of the quiet into the trembling air. I come to parts where no light shines.

CANTO V

Thus I went down from the first circle to the second one, that takes less room and has more grief, pricking to woe. There Minos is, and horror with him as he snarls. He stands within its entrance to examine faults; he judges men and sends them down according as he wraps himself. I say, that when the ill-born soul comes before Minos, it gives full confession; and he, who knows all sins, sees what is fitting place in hell for it. He girds himself about then with his tail as many times as makes the number of the circles that it must descend. Many are in front of him always; each takes his turn for judgment; they speak and hear, and down they go. 'O you who come to this abode of grief,' said Minos to me when he saw me first, leaving the exercise of his great office, 'look how you come and whom you trust! Let not the entrance, by its width, deceive you! . . .' And my guide to him: 'Why do you shout? Hinder not his fated way: it is willed so where what one wishes, that one can. So ask no more.' Now sorrowing notes begin to press upon my ear; now I have come where sounds of weeping meet me. I came into a place dead to all light, moaning like a stormy sea when it is beaten by opposing winds. The squall of hell, which never stops, carries the spirits with it as it goes, turning and striking them to do them hurt. And when they come before the ruin, here are shrieks, wailing, laments; and here they rail upon God's worth. I learnt that carnal sinners are so damned, for putting reason after their desire. And as the starlings wing in broad full flocks in winter-time, so did the wind carry these bad spirits. Here, and there, down, and up, it takes them. No hope gives comfort ever either of rest, or even lesser pain. And as the cranes go, chanting their lays, in long lines through the air, so did I see come, making lament, shades that were carried by the wind along. And so I said: 'Master, who are these so punished by black air?' 'The first of those of whom you wish to know,' he answered then, 'was empress over many peoples. She was so broken to the vice of lust that in her law she made all licit that might be desired, to take the blame away she had incurred. Semiramis is she, of whom one reads she followed Ninus and was as well his bride. Hers was the land the Soldan now corrects. The next is she who killed herself for love, breaking her promise to Sicheus' ashes. Then comes the lustful Cleopatra.

See Helen, for whom so long, so cruelly men fought, and see the great Achilles who fought at last with love. See Paris, Tristram'; more than a thousand shades he pointed out, naming them all, whom love cut off from this our life. When I had heard my teacher name the ancient ladies and the knights, pity came on me, mazing me almost. I began: 'Poet, willingly would I speak with those two who go together, and seem so light upon the wind.' And he to me: 'You shall see when they are near to us; then beg them by that love which carries them, and they will come.' Soon as the wind bore them towards us I spoke to them: 'O souls in your distress, come here and speak with us, if another stops you not!' As doves called by desire, with still poised wings, come through the air carried by their will to their sweet nest, so from the throng where Dido is they came to us through the malignant air, so strong was my affectionate cry. 'O gracious, kindly creature, visiting through this dark air us who stained the world with blood, if the world's king were friend to us, then we would pray him for your peace, since you take pity on our cruel lot. We will hear and speak to you of what you wish to hear and speak, what time the wind, as now, is stilled for us. The city of my birth is on the shore where Po comes down to peace with all his followers. Love, that is quickly learnt by gentle hearts, took hold of this man for the beauty that was taken from me; and the way offends me still. Love, that lets no loved one off from love, took hold of me in liking him so much, that, as you see, it still is with me yet. Love brought us to one death: Cain waits for him who took our lives away.' These words were uttered by them to us, and hearing these offended souls, I bent my head and held it down so long that at the last the poet said: 'What are you thinking?' When I replied, I said, 'Alas, how sweet the thoughts, how much desire, that led these to their grievous end!' And then I turned to them and said: 'Francesca, your sufferings make me sad and near to tears. But tell me: when your sighs were sweet, how and why did love allow you knowledge of doubtful desires?' And she to me: 'There is no greater grief than to recall one's happiness in one's own misery; and this your teacher knows. But if you feel for us so much to wish to know the first roots of our love, then I will do as one who weeps and speaks. We read one day for our delight of Lancelot, when love caught hold of him. We were alone, and unsuspecting. And several times our reading made our eyes to meet, and turned our faces pale; but one page only conquered us. For when we read about that smile so much desired, and kissed by such a lover, this man, who never shall be torn apart from me, all trembling kissed my lips. A pandar was the book, and he who wrote it. That day we read no more.' While the one spirit spoke these words, the other wept, so that I swooned with pity just as one who dies. I fell as a dead body falls.

C

DANTE'S JOURNEY

DANTE'S JOURNEY

AT the beginning of the eighteenth century the chance sinking of a well near Naples reached the ruins of Herculaneum, at ninety feet below the surface. It might have seemed to be an exciting find, and yet they proceeded to inspect the site with Neapolitan slowness, and one can read in travellers' accounts of the descent down endless lava-steps into the gloom of the candle-lit excavations, where the faint light wavered on the theatre or on a temple, while up above the sun shone on a new town. And when the matter was handed over to the erudite, for explanation, there were dangers also. The King of Naples called in one Baiardi, a man with more than all the apparatus needed for the task

> (On voit bien qu'il a lu, mais ce n'est pas l'affaire;
> Qu'il cache son savoir, et montre son esprit!)

and appetite enough to show it off. 'Baiardi, that vast and inde-fatigable compiler, respectable from the qualities of his heart, and terrible by his memory to those who hear him talk or venture to read him, had cultivated every species of literature, and collected in his head an enormous though undigested mass of knowledge, which escaped from him confusedly. He set out with a general catalogue of the remains preserved at Portici, in one volume folio; and as the engravings, which should represent them, were not yet ready, he obtained the king's permission, to place at the head of the great commentary a preface, intended to point out the epoch, the consequences and the use of the researches at Herculaneum. He published the first part of this work in *seven volumes quarto*, without having entered upon his subject.'

Now the world of Dante lies more than ninety feet below the pavements of our modern world, and it would be possible for me (had I Baiardi's terrible memory, and indefatigable industry) to give a preface to the commentary of Dante to rival those seven volumes quarto, and without entering on the subject either. We have only to turn over the pages of the catalogues to the Dante collections to see how the lava has flowed over him, and left him buried amidst the commentaries. How could it be

29

otherwise? Homer or Virgil had a story to tell, but Dante had a world to explain, in the light of ideas which seemed to him to govern it; and he had as well another world to explore, one that we are less familiar with now. All that is something complicated, even at its origin, and it is remote. And yet I feel that few would thank me overmuch for volumes of commentary, however I protested in producing them that they were legitimate, or even indispensable. It is better for me to plunge down the shaft that we have opened with the beginning of the *Inferno*, and to give some idea of what lies buried, not by candlelight, but as though it was all open to the eye. For these reasons, and also because I am anxious to move forward to the consideration of Dante as being a different sort of poet from Virgil (whom he thought his teacher, and whom he made his guide), I shall say as little of the circumstances as I can, and as much of the poem itself.

The *Divine Comedy* is the poem of the world gone wrong. The pilgrim Dante, and he represents you or me, man in general, sees the world of his own time plunged in confusion. The factions of his native Florence lead to Dante's exile, and in the bitter exercise of climbing other people's stairs and the salt taste of other people's bread Dante thinks over both what is, and what should be. He isolates himself from his fellow-exiles as much as from his opponents; he makes a party of himself, and from that party-platform he writes his poem. The wood with which we have seen the *Divine Comedy* opening is the symbol of a world out of order: it is trackless, and dark, and wrong. For there are two ways of looking at the cruel muddle of the world: we may take it that it is a chaos that has always been, and out of which we might by our exertions and our intelligence create some order, even though that order might be local or temporary. That is the answer of Machiavelli and of the humanists, one in which order lies before us rather than behind because it is what man creates and not a portion of the universe. Or we may say that the muddle comes because the world has left the pattern in which, and in which alone, it was right. That is the answer of Dante and the medievals, and it is one in which order lies behind us, even more than it lies in front. For there is then no certainty that we shall mend our ways and keep our place, but there is a certainty that there was a place for us to keep. How is Dante's attitude to be distinguished from that of the Renascence? Touch them at this point, and they will fall on opposite sides of the line: with the Renascence we shall go forward to the creation of civilization, which is the proper work of man; with Dante, we are to go back from the muddle which is man's to the order, which was God's.

If that is so, it follows that the order is clearly legislated for, and that the steps away from it are as obvious as they are fatal. Nothing, then, is more characteristic of Dante than this fact that he owes absolute allegiance to certain authorities which are, within their several fields, the sovereign arbiters of the world as it should be. There is Aristotle, who is its Philosopher *par excellence*; there is the Pope who is its spiritual head, and who leads forward to the proper goal of eternal felicity, and by his side there is the Emperor who is its temporal head, who holds in check the wilfulness of man, and leads, in the right ordering of the active life, to temporal felicity. Let either of these last be absent from his place, or faulty in his action, and the pattern of the world is spoilt. It is the double tragedy of 1300, in Dante's view of it, that both sides are defective. There is no universal Emperor to guide the world aright, and keep it one. And whom have we seen, in the first canto of the *Inferno*, stand ready to aid Dante when he is distressed by all the obstacles that keep him from progress in the active life? It is Virgil, the poet of Augustus. Virgil is Dante's guide for the plainest reason: because he is the singer of the Universal Empire which is the summit of human achievement before the Redemption, and the providential disposition after it. Aeneas and David, in Dante's view, stand as contemporaries and heads of parallel lines: the progeny of the one will culminate in the representatives of Empire, that of the other in the founder of the Church, and the two institutions are both sacrosanct. But therefore Virgil, in his first appearance to Dante, is weak from long silence, because for fifty years no Emperor has applied himself to the task of keeping the world in its right way. Therefore, there is no possibility for the right living of the active life, for Dante's time, or for Dante himself, until such time at least as the Emperor shall resume his function and his place. But because such is the plan that governs the universe, then this return to the order which is right can be the first prophecy of the *Inferno* as it opens.

It is not only the Empire which is absent, it is the Papacy which is warped from its mission. Dante is the supreme believer in the medieval ideals, of Empire and of Papacy; but what is wrong with the Middle Ages, for him, is that they have not been fulfilled. They should both be equal and independent, ruling in harmony separate spheres of human life. Yet they have always been in contest, and now while the Emperor is missing, the Pope has usurped his office, and this second flaw is as fatal in its consequences as the first. Of the three beasts who stay Dante's progress in the first canto of the *Inferno* the last, and worst, is the she-wolf who symbolizes the grasping avarice of the papal curia. An Emperor once had turned his back on Rome and on the west, leaving as his temporal heir one who had no writ to think of temporal things. 'Ah Constantine, to how much ill was mother, not your conversion, but the dowry which the first rich Father took from you!'[1] And from that Donation of the Emperor Constantine derives the papal meddling in temporal things, a deviation leading all too fast to despiritualization and corruption. The burden of Dante's attack against the papacy, and it will be constant and biting through his poem, lies just here, that there is no going right until the Pope has retreated within the limits of his jurisdiction. The world is wrong, because both its heads are wrong. What, in this plight, can Dante do? First, he can be sure that Providence does not mean it so, and he can set out the recipe so that men can recapture it. He may plead with the Emperor, and scourge the Pope; and turning aside from the active life which is denied to him, as to all other men, he may pass to contemplation of the rules which govern the world, in order to persuade back to what should, and indeed, must, be. And in pursuit of that, he may push his contemplation to its lawful goal: if this world is denied us, is there not still the next which is its commentary and its completion? It is the necessary journey which Virgil proposes to Dante at the end of Canto I.

Such is the situation at the outset of the *Divine Comedy*; such the reasons for the journey through the supernatural world proposed to Dante in this initial and prefatory canto which completes the number of the whole in this most rigorously architectural of all great poems. The divisions of the poem are three, the cantos in each division thirty-three, and three times

[1] *Inf.* XIX, 115–7.

thirty-three plus one gives the perfect number of a hundred to the whole. Is not the metre also based on the same play of threes and ones? and this, like the subdivisions of the separate canticles, has its theological significance. And even if we do not share the medieval interest in the symbolism of numbers, we cannot rate it as anything but fortunate that Dante knows so supremely from the beginning where he is going, and how, and why. For it is not only the numbers which are clear, it is the way as well. The plan of Dante's universe, as it is presented by the *Comedy*, is beautiful in its simplicity. It is the fall of Lucifer which first created sin, and thereby also created hell. His crash opened the funnel within the earth on whose circumference are the contracting circles of the *Inferno*, and at the centre is the author of it all, Lucifer himself, in endless impotence. On him, as it is right, there bears down the crushing weight of all the rocks that form the scaffolding of hell; to him there flow down all the tears of all the world, which form the final unity of all the rivers of hell. Nothing, said Virgil, in all that Dante has seen is more notable than this, and it is the confirmation of order in the distant past. 'In the middle of the sea there is a rotten land,' he said, 'which is called Crete, under whose king the world was one time chaste. There is a mountain there, Ida by name, that once was gay with waters and with leaves: now it is desert like some worn-out thing.'[1] And here in Crete stands the colossus with its head of gold, and its declining metals down to iron and earthenware, all split except the head, and oozing tears which flow through Acheron, Styx and Phlegethon to form at last Cocytus. Save at its origin, in the nobility of that golden head, the action of the world is cracked, and the tears of its wrongness drain away, down to the author Lucifer. But Lucifer himself is subordinated— who more?—to the rule of three: with his three faces he is the anti-trinity, the vanishing-point of life as of intelligence. He had been created spirit without matter, now he is only matter without spirit. His blank faces have no function, other than to maul the supreme traitors who should be his chiefest favourites: Brutus and Cassius, who betrayed the Empire; Judas Iscariot, who betrayed the Church. His bat's wings chill the air with an icy wind which is the antithesis of Pentecost, freezing the waters as they fall. Dante, we have seen, was unable to give account of how he came

[1] *Inf.* XIV, 85–90.

into the wood of sin, because he left the way in sleep. Sleep is the symbol of error, and error persisted in leads on to deeper sleep and death, to the final disappearance of the mind, to the sheet of ice where the last sinners are entombed, and where the only action left is this senseless one of Lucifer, condemned eternally to chew his foremost followers.

The tears of the world, I said, fall as the rivers of hell to lose their movement in Cocytus. There is a unity in them, and there is a unity too, in Dante's view, in the fatal progression of evil to which they act accompaniment. This also is foreshadowed from the beginning in the three beasts which we have seen turn Dante back. They are the opening trinity of evil, as Lucifer is the concluding one of hell; for there are three stages in our undoing, and they are also one. We shall begin with incontinence in our appetites: that is the edge of hell, before the city of Dis. Is it Love that is incontinent? it may not lack attraction, or nobility; and we have seen Dante himself swoon when he heard Francesca's words. But let it be Ciacco's greedy guzzling only one step further on, and we and Dante feel only repulsion and contempt. Ciacco's greed for food brings Dante to the greed of his and Ciacco's birthplace, Florence, and to the first of a series of fierce invective. 'Upstarts and sudden profits have produced, Florence, in you, such over-weening pride that you already weep for it.'[1] And soon the canto of Ulysses will begin significantly with the grim apostrophe to Florence: 'Florence, rejoice, that you have grown so great you flap your wings by land and sea, and spread your name abroad in Hell!'[2] For obviously, where the right order of the active life is missing, Florence can only prosper at her peril, breeding appetites which mean undoing. Nor is that true of Florence only, all equally may find it true, and the more they have given rein to appetite, the more fatal will they find it: 'How many think themselves up there great kings, who shall be here as swine in mire, leaving behind them horrible contempt!'[3] All action if it is not right—and right it cannot be without the frame is right—is wrong; and the incontinence of our appetite, though in itself it offends God least, yet leads us on, and down. How shall we satisfy the cravings of our appetite, if not by violence? To the first depravation we shall have added then its fellow: the will follows the appetite. Nor

[1] *Inf.* XVI, 73–5.   [2] *Inf.* XXVI, 1–3.   [3] *Inf.* VIII, 49–51.

shall we stop there, though in this trinity of evil there is one step only further to be made. 'Injury is the end of every act of malice which wins hatred in heaven, and every injury saddens other men by force or fraud.'[1] From the depravation of the appetite proceeds, as fatal consequence, the depravation of the will; and from the depravation of the will, that of the mind itself. So we descend inevitably to the bottom and the worst, where 'in the smallest circle, at the point of the universe where sits Lucifer, whoever has betrayed for ever is consumed.'[2]

Dante's mind ran naturally to symbols and to allegory, a process which can often give depth, even if it also gives difficulties. Nor did he leave this central business of the progressive depravation of man without its tokens. Look in the opening cantos of *Inferno* where appetite alone is wrong, and you will find, for instance, those birds that recur conspicuously in Canto V. They are single in their nature. But when we reach incontinence of anger, and reach as well the level of Dis itself, while Dante and Virgil pause excluded from the hostile city, the Furies from the battlements threaten Dante with Medusa. Let her be doubt, or heresy, there is no difficulty in that: but she is also, for the first time, dual in her nature, human but with hair of snakes. That is no accident, and her compeers follow her. When we pass within the walls of Dis we find first the tombs that break the country-side as heresy breaks the unity of the Church: tombs and the fire that filled them, and the lids hanging waiting for more occupants until the count is filled and the world ends. And then we come to Violence, and find the centaurs set as guardians to the circle, while on its threshold lies the Minotaur. Partly, it is that their whole tradition linked the centaurs with acts of violence, and in that context the Minotaur's name speaks for itself. But it is not an accident that these are double-natured also, for we have added a complication in our progress down; and there is still one more to come. 'Many are those animals with which she weds,' we saw of the she-wolf, and it is the formula of depravation. Let greed join with fraud, it will be usury, or simony; let fraud endeavour satisfaction for lust, it will be procuration, or falsification of persons, and here, where there are snakes but no ladders, we shall slither down. And at the centre-piece of hell we meet the figure which rises out of the circle of the fraudulent, casting

[1] *Inf.* XI, 22-4.   [2] *ibid.*, 64-6.

a blandishing eye towards the circle of the Violent, while with its forked and venomous tail it dominates the abyss down which the waters crash, and where, deep in their misery, are the ten divisions of Malebolge, the realm of fraud before the final dolorous realm of treachery.

This is an episode which, in its details, used to puzzle the commentators, and which they now have solved. Dante and Virgil have descended through the incontinent and the violent; they are on the edge of the pit which breaks the continuity of the funnel, and there is no way on. At this emergency Virgil takes from Dante the cord with which he had been girt, and by virtue of which he had once thought to tame the leopard who signified incontinence: and this last may be Dante's confession that in his youth he had been on the point of becoming a Franciscan. But Virgil bundles the cord as something of no value, and chucks it down into the abyss. Once, in the time of St. Francis, it could stand for chastity; but in the degeneracy of time it stands for something else, not for a virtue, but for the show of virtue with the reality of vice: it is hypocrisy. When Dante put it on first in his youth, he thought it efficacious; but seeing so many clerics damned in hell, he knows its insufficiency. It is something to throw away, for the reed of true humility to take its place on the shores of purgatory. So sharp is Dante's indignation against those whose way lies most clear, and yet who leave it. But meanwhile the cord of hypocrisy is the fit summons to call a monster from the vasty deep, and out of the realm of Fraud a creature rises in answer to the bait. At first it seems human, like a diver distorted by the water; then it is a beast; then come its details, its face, the face of a just man, its body serpentine, its claws, those of a lion. It lies to like a boat; or like a beaver, with its tail dipped in the water to entice the fish. And then there comes its name: it is Geryon, *forma tricorporis umbrae*, the threefold monster who adds the last corruption, and adds as well the final complication beyond that of the centaurs. We are at the mathematical centre of the *Inferno* when Virgil breaks out in exclamation at the presence, and the power, of Fraud. 'Here is the beast with the pointed tail, that passes the hills and breaks the walls and man's defence; here is the beast which stinks through all the world!'[1]

[1] *Inf.* XVII, 1–3.

Incontinence, Violence, Fraud, this is the trinity of Dante's hell, divided and anatomized down the shrinking circles of the pit. Such is the simple outline of the *Inferno*. Were there enough, in the Middle Ages, to pour into this drain? We have seen already the answer to the question in Canto III. The world has not gone right, its error dates as far at least as Constantine, and in such circumstances the gates of Purgatory will be rusty from disuse, while Hell knows no shortage of inhabitants. And we can discern, in Dante's treatment of the throng in Canto III, a general method. Those, in the vestibule of hell, were those who never ventured to take sides, the pusillanimous, the trimmers, those who kept their precious skins intact. We can feel the blast of Dante's scorn for them. So full is his contempt that justice does not stay to give a name to them. They are a blank crowd, rushing headlong after a blank banner, always in movement, yet for nothing!—they who did not incommode themselves in life whatever was the cause. They neglected in their life all stimulus to good, and now their only stimulus is that of insects' stings. They treasured up their precious blood, and now it falls in drops that feed only loathsome worms. They shunned pain, and now it causes tears which evoke no pity; and Dante merely looks away. *In quo iudicio iudicaveritis, iudicamini, et in qua mensura mensi fueritis remetietur vobis.* It is the law which Aquinas called the *contrappassum* which normally holds for the punishments of hell; and it is the method we shall see in one of those grand scenes of the *Inferno* where Dante vents his anger against the man who is supremely wrong because he ought to be supremely right—'il gran prete—a cui mal prenda!'[1] Boniface VIII looms often up behind the surface of Dante's poetry, and nowhere more than in the bolgia of the simoniacs. The descent via Geryon has been made, the realm of Fraud with the concentric circles of Malebolge has been entered, and already we have sampled in the second bolgia, with the bemerded flatterers, the energy of Dante's own reaction. Down in the next ditch, with feet protruding from holes that seem like tombs, are those who made a traffic out of sacred things. They filled their purses on the earth, and now they are a filling. They turned upside down the law of the gospel, and they are themselves inverted. They loved too well the goods of the earth, and into it they are now stuck. 'And

---

[1] *Inf.* XXVII, 70.

as a flame on greasy things moves only on the outer husk, so was it there from heel to tip of toe.'[1] These flames which burn the feet of the simoniacs are grimly reminiscent of the tongues of fire of Pentecost, something less, and more, than a halo. And if Boniface can not be here in person, yet he is expected eagerly. There is no coincidence in the fact that *eight* cantos further on we shall come back to the cry of Guido da Montefeltro which I have quoted against the Pope, 'il gran prete—a cui mal prenda.' And since this world is wrong right from its centre there is one consequence which we may draw already anticipatorily. In so far as human activity is recorded in the *Divine Comedy* it is wrong activity: the right activity appears as a symbol in the gold head of Crete that we have seen. It is possible: but what would it be? Dante never saw the need, or found the place, to make an answer to this question. But we, who must return to this again, may do so for him. His view of right activity must be one which involves the innocency of human relationships without envisaging any purely human increment that derives from these. What is humanism but the thickening of the belt of human activity (the thoughts that man has thought, the poetry man has written, the buildings man has made, the paintings man has created) until it affords a living-space for man? But how should this suit Dante's book? His aim can never be to enrich the present, to enhance its significance, or to increase its hold: but Dante himself will never be aware of this, because he is too preoccupied with the wrongness of the present to realize that he has no place, and no need, to think of it in terms of construction. Let us step outside this world for just a moment. There is in one of Mlle de Scudéry's portraits a detail which the Renascence would have recognized, and Dante not: 'Elle aime les belles choses, et les connoist, comme la Musique, la Poësie, et la Peinture, quoy qu'elle soit d'un tempera- ment un peu melancolique, elle inspire pourtant une ioye à ceux qui luy parlent, et sans qu'il paroisse qu'elle y songe, elle gagne bien tost le coeur de ceux qui l'approchent.'[2] That is very simple in its statement of the interests of Europe for several centuries. But we have only to place it by this episode of Nicholas III, with its burden of indignation against Boniface, to see that it belongs to another world; and to realize that the old arguments about Dante being the last of the medievals, or first

---

[1] *Inf.* XIX, 28-30.   [2] *Clélie*, IV, III, 858.

of the moderns, blanketed the point. The human relationships
of the *Inferno*, in that they are wrong, are on the minus side of
zero; and when we get to *Purgatorio* we shall find our gaze goes
elsewhere. That is why rightness—which for Dante is something
only hypothetical, is also something only mechanical, a lubrica-
tion of the elements by which the world works, so that we
work right and wait well for our transference to what is more
our business. For Dante's Emperor may not be subject to his
Pope: but both are equally subject to his God, nor could man's
activity be other than *ancilla theologiae*. Does not that explain
enough the blank there is on this one side? the fact that his
Emperor when in his place changes everything, yet changes
nothing? How so? It is an alchemy which comes, not through
this or that being different by virtue of achievement, but from
all relations being right, instead of being wrong. Instead with
Mlle de Scudéry's portrait we were on the plus side of zero:
what was, was an addition to be reckoned with and counted on,
not a subtraction to be deplored. It is this simple, but important,
difference that makes her discount Dante as much as Lady
Politick Would-be. 'Tu vois d'abord le premier Poëte Italien dont
on parlera un iour, mais regarde le comme un homme qui choi-
sira une matiere difficile á traiter en vers, et qui s'expliquera si
obscurement qu'à peine sera t'il entendu par ceux de son siecle.
Il naistra à une ville qui se nommera Florence, il s'appellera
Dante, et sera peu veritable en ses escrits.'[1] Is that ignorance, or
flippancy? It may, as a particular passage in a particular writer,
be either of those, according to our private view of the merits of
Sapho; but it is also the symbol of two different, and uncompre-
hending, worlds. And in that context Sapho speaks the language
of several centuries.

We have digressed from travelling into argument, a thing
which Dante also did, and did increasingly as he advanced: so
that I may plead his example, and offer him as warning. For it is
my purpose to go on from the examination of Dante's theme to
the consideration of Dante's poetry; and to that our assessment of
his meaning is strictly relevant. But if we go back again, we may
feel confident we know the reason why Dante, in Canto XVI
of each of his three canticles, looks backward for the exercise
of virtues, seeing them in a generation that has gone. And we

[1] *Clélie*, IV, II, 559.

may note confirmation of what we have seen. For here Dante is most explicit in what he requires above the line, instead of damning what he finds beneath it; and there is a pair which links the cantos close together: 'valore e cortesia,' 'cortesia e valor.'[1] Do you like Shelley, or Robert Browning? Poussin or Van Gogh? Henry Moore or Bernini? *Il s'agit bien de cela*, and such a question might be put by Amiclée to Melinthe, not by Dante to the better generations that are gone. Round him there is change and decay, that corresponds to political misdirection. Before him there was, or so he deems there was, modesty, sober manners, the liberal and knightly virtues of our ancestors. There are fraudulent counsellors in Malebolge, but there is no other counsel as to positive activity than this. That is quite logical: as logical as the linking of the theme of Ulysses, with his knowledge acquired in pride and egoism, with that of Florence, grown rich in useless trade. The names of Florence and Ulysses spread equally through hell. We, looking from outside, and with the privileges of the onlooker, may see achievement in the alterations of Florentine government in the second half of the thirteenth century. We may see the Medici on the horizon, the basis for accomplishment being laid. But Dante saw otherwise. And naturally, as we press down the funnel, into the pathology of Malebolge, it is the wrongness that is accentuated. Look at Maestro Adamo, the last of the great figures among the fraudulent. On him all the corruption of the century converges: a century that had seen, for Dante, the overturning of the moral sense, the dissolution of the religious spirit which had been stricken to death by simony, and was soon to agonize at Avignon; and that had seen as well the political crumbling away. Maestro Adamo is the symbol of economic ruin in a society rendered degenerate by immoderate ambition and luxury, as by the bad example set by those who should have been the pattern of noble rectitude—whether they are Boniface himself, or as more immediately here, the feudal nobles who were above him. That is why Malebolge smells so foul, and is so lurid. Here the floor is stone, and may give place to mud or pitch, or be broken by deep holes. Here it is lit by flames, here reddened by blood. Now it is like a field of battle, now a plague-stricken hospital, now a desert full of deadly snakes. Are there men here? Then they will

---

[1] *Purg.* XVI, 116, and *Inf.* XVI, 67.

appear, like Ugolino, in some horrid detail only, with animal mouth wiped on a gnawed and bloody scalp. And so we shall pass down to the 'emperor of the grievous realm,'

L'imperador del doloroso regno,

embattled at the centre of it all, where are as well the traitors to the supreme authorities set up by God, and where—after the fossils in the ice—the death of society marches with the death of the spirit; and Dante and Virgil can start at last their strenuous climb away from hell, up to the shore, and to the stars.

There is a principle which Dante sets himself in the *Paradiso*, and which I have tried to follow: 'This cry of yours shall do as does the wind, which strikes the highest summits of the hills; and that shall be no little argument of honour. Therefore there are shown to you within these wheels, on the mount of Purgatory and in the sorrowing valley, those souls only which are known to fame; for the mind of the hearer does not pause, nor stay its faith for an example whose root is hidden and unknown, nor for any argument that is not evident.'[1] Or as another poet puts it,

'Tis the taught already profit by teaching,

and we learn easily only those things which we know. But because of that, the principle was easier to apply in dealing with the *Inferno* than it is with Purgatory or Paradise. Hell, which is things gone wrong, and the punishment of things gone wrong, is, as we know too well, something self-evident. It is not only the inhabitants of Dante's hell who live 'down in the world of endless bitterness,'

Giú ne lo mondo sanza fine amaro,

and we know our way instinctively into the pit. But Dante's Purgatory is something different, and we must measure the gap between his knowledge of the universe and our own before we can envisage it. For Dante one half the world (it is our own) is land, and has inhabitants. The southern hemisphere stretches with unbroken sea. Only, at the antipodes to Jerusalem, there rises up one isolated mount, shaped like a cone, but flattened at the top. To it no living man can come, or if he comes, it is

---

[1] *Par.* XVII, 133–142.

D

like the Ulysses we saw, who comes with all his pride, and then makes shipwreck only after sighting it.

The mount of Purgatory, set at this distance, in these unknown, and unreal, seas, has something of the quality of a mirage for us, now that we have filled the oceans with other lands, and no Eldorados beckon. And even for Dante it is beyond the range of visual intensity. And so it should be, perhaps: for here, in this mysterious island, in this ocean of solitude, we are to begin the passage from physical to spiritual reality, and all the outlines have to blur and fade. The sights, the sounds, the stench of hell—these are all tangible. They can be presented in the most authentic vision; and as well we are always looking back to the surface of the world, and to this present life, which is the sole reality known to the damned. But from Purgatory, which is a hill, up which we climb, we look onwards, not behind. Onwards, and upwards: into light and space. In this infinity there is not even a mountain to arrest the eye, nothing but an overplus of brilliance to dim, or blind, its seeing. And what here is human personality, which towered with Farinata or with Ulysses? It is what we have left behind. Soon we shall look, and doubt whether we see at all. It is the case of Dante with the souls of Paradise. 'As through transparent polished glass, or through waters bright and still, but not so deep to make the bottom dark, the image of our faces comes back weak, so that a pearl on a white brow comes no less quickly to our eye, so there I saw faces ready to speak to us . . .'[1] What we know dwindles, till we see faces, instead of seeing men. And what of the things we do not know, into whose realm we are advancing? They are by essence the unseen and the unimaginable, and as we proceed through *Paradiso* we shall find the way strewn with Dante's confessions of inadequacy of vision; or if his eyes were equal to the view, yet it exceeds his utterance. 'From this time on what I saw was more than our speech shows, which yields before such vision; and memory yields because it was outraged.'[2] It is not an accident that men have fastened most upon *Inferno* as the legacy of Dante: partly it may be laziness, for we more often begin than finish the *Divine Comedy*. But it is partly also because hell represents all men's experience, while purgatory and paradise are instead all men's inexperience; and Dante with all his stature cannot hide that state of things.

[1] *Par.* III, 10–15.   [2] *Par.* XXXIII, 55–7.

I have started by spreading the mist before the reader's eyes, and should perhaps do something next to scatter it. For the simplicity of which I spoke obtains in purgatory as much as hell, and we have not left the world of sense-impressions. Even, there is something exhilarating in this conception which is Dante's contribution to the idea of the supernatural world. Lucifer, we saw, was the prime origin of sin, and buried under it; reduced, not in bulk, but in intelligence, till in his blankness he serves as the providential instrument for the punishment of those three traitors to whom he owes the greatest honours. This, as we may reckon it, is the plain opposite of Milton's Lucifer. The latter marshals his forces, and cons the future:

> What though the field be lost?
> All is not lost; th'unconquerable will,
> And study of revenge, immortal hate
> And courage never to submit or yield,
> And what is else not to be overcome.

There is not sufficient articulation in the empty bulk of Dante's Lucifer to string those boasts together. He is a negation, not a potentate or a general; and the supreme dismissal of what he stands for lies in the fact that he is as well the instrument of providence for the creation of purgatory. For the mount of purgatory is the cone of displacement which compensates for the cone of hell. The fall of Lucifer drives in the pit, and out the mountain, on whose shores Dante and Virgil have emerged at last.

All the time they had remained hidden in the bowels of the earth there was no mention of the sun, from the first canto when Dante was driven backwards from its light. That is a natural consequence of being underground; but it has as well its symbolism. The sun for Dante represents the light of grace, and only when he reaches the shore of purgatory can it rise again. The dawn of hope is breaking in the eastern sky. Henceforth it will shine, and its light increase, until it is itself reached and surpassed in paradise. Meanwhile, what of the place into which the two travellers have come? It is easier even to summarize than hell: there, in the progression of evil, I abbreviated the task. Some categories I omitted, and I left out the controversial matter of what system Dante may have followed, or invented. But here all is clear, and orthodox. We may abandon sin, and yet the inclination and the warp of it remain: and in purgatory, since penitence has intervened, there is no sin to punish, but there are these remnants of it to be expunged. It is only when they are gone that the will to go forward is resumed. This is a question, then, of sin in its essence, not in its social consequence, and hence the simple basing of the arrangement of purgatory upon the capital sins. In hell sin gathered gravity as we went down; here we go up towards the lesser faults. At the bottom of the seven is Pride; then Envy, Anger. Then by one of Dante's symmetries, the centrepiece of purgatory is taken up with his theory of love in its two divisions, the sort that is instinctive, and the other of the mind. It is the counterpart to the centre of hell, which was taken up with fraud. All actions spring from love, and if they have gone wrong, it is through love misplaced; and that is Pride, Envy and Wrath; or else it is this central circle of insufficient love, a sluggishness in following the true good; or after that, it is excessive love for earthly goods. So the last circles of the mount are left to Avarice, Gulosity and Lust, and we are back where we had entered on the downward path in hell.

The circles of Purgatory, then, are few, and we may ask: if Dante gives to each a canto, or even if he gives them two, where does he find the matter for the canticle? The answer is, that there are four primary divisions to the mount of purgatory (that is, three, plus one): there is the shore from which the pilgrims start; there is the ante-purgatory; and after purgatory itself, on the flat surface of the beheaded cone, there is the Earthly Paradise. We have seen already, by anticipation, the action that is to take place on the shores of purgatory. Dante had given to Virgil the useless cord that girt him to be thrown down as a lure to Geryon. Here, when Virgil has washed his cheeks clean of the stain of hell, he girds Dante in its place with the reed of true humility, humility, which is the beginning of penitence. Girt with humility, washed clean of worldly desires, Dante is ready to proceed. At the opening of the canto it was the pause before the dawn: now after these preliminaries Grace can show the way of perfection and of happiness. The canto ends with the miracle of the reed that springs again where Virgil plucked it out; for it is an urgent truth with Dante, both that the means of salvation are inexhaustible, and that while human goods are limited and consumable—so that what you have is what I have not—moral good is inconsumable, communicable to all beyond all limit. Let it be money,

A has it, *therefore* B has it not. But let it be humility, or charity:
A's does not hinder B's, but may beget it. Or we might even
say, A has it, *therefore* B can have it too. It is an idea which
Dante will make later into theory—an idea, I dare not say a truth,
for on both sides it may need qualifying. Nothing is sadder, or
surer, in this world than that humility begets insolence, and
charity, abuse and imposition. 'And wo unto him who living in
all submissness with an humorous Master, hath not heart enough
so to resent himself once a year, as may turn injuries into better
observances: Nor are we burthen-bearing beasts more beaten
than Mules are, for any other reason but that they are excellently
well skil'd in kicking, whilst we patiently undergo the lash;
and you know much better than I, Beroaldo, that in these times
with Masters, *Nihil profici patientia, nisi ut graviora, tanquam ex
facili tolerantibus imperentur.'*[1] And on the other hand, if Lord
Nuffield has a motor-car, that fact may aid, and not prevent,
our having one as well. Nor will it, as in the case of humility-
insolence, be an anti-motor-car which we receive. In other
words, physical goods may be more communicable than spiritual
ones. But these reflections are not Dante's, and with this
replenishment of the reed the canto closes. With the second
one's beginning the sun has already risen on the scene of purgatory. Dante and Virgil can seek their way.

The gate of purgatory proper is up the mountain-side, and the
part before it is the place of pause for those who have been
negligent in fulfilling religious duties: those who were excom-
municate, those who were indolent, those who suffering violent
death repented only when it came upon them. Here Dante
meets with Manfred, the heir of the great Emperor, Frederick II,
and can give expression to his enthusiasm for their imperial policy.
'And one of them began: "Whoever you are, so going, turn
your face; think if you ever saw me over there." I turned towards
him, and gazed upon him hard: fair he was and beautiful, and
noble in his air . . .' Dante had looked before, and his look was an
indictment. Now we are in a new world where it can signify
affection, and can caress its object; and it invests Manfred with a
royal dignity. For above all Manfred is here as one who almost
had achieved his father's purpose, and stood forth as King of
Italy and as Emperor. Had he won, Frederick's conception of

[1] *Advertisements from Parnassus*, II, XCIII, 314.

the State might have been given body, as a supreme entity, master of all, and based on law and justice, keeping in check the ambition of men and parties, preventing civil strife, so that all moved within the State, through the State, and according to the will of the State. But Manfred died, and Dante's dream of a world-order under a world-Emperor was deferred, to wait on providence. Since providence had decreed it, Dante's hope in individuals can wax and wane, without his sureness failing. Could it be out of the divine plan for the world to have its order? Since God is one must not the world politically be one? Dante's answer is constant throughout the *Comedy*: it comes in the epithet *good* which he gives to the Roman emperors by virtue of their office; it comes in the exaltation of the imperial eagle, the *sacred bird* whose apotheosis we shall find in paradise, as in the constant symmetry of Church and Empire, the two universal institutions which are meant to hold the world aright.

Yet it is here, unless I am mistaken, that there arises a quite logical illogicality in Dante, something that he never budgeted for, and yet could not avoid; something again that underlines for us his being of the Middle Ages, and outside the Renascence. Of the four divisions of the mountain I have so far only barely mentioned one, the flat summit of the cone which forms the Earthly Paradise. There was a tradition amongst the theologians which pushed it out into the distant spaces of the seas, but Dante's extrusion of purgatory from underground, with his superimposition on it of the Earthly Paradise is his original contribution. There is still a barrier of flames around the Garden of Eden, they are those which purge the lustful in the last circle of purgatory, and through them (fire being the essential element of purgation) Dante and Virgil pass to reach it. Then all the ladder of the mount is scaled, and Virgil's office as guide is at its term. 'Then Virgil fixed his eyes on me and said: "You have seen, my son, the temporal and the eternal fire, and you have come into a place where I discern no further by myself. I have brought you here with skill and art: now take your pleasure as your guide, for you are out of steep ways, out of narrow ones. You see the sun that shines upon your brow; you see the grass, the flowers and the trees, which here the earth produces by itself. Until those lovely eyes shall come in happiness which, weeping, made me come to you, you may sit or you may go amongst

them as you please. Wait not now my saying nor my nod: your will is whole, upright and free, and it would be an error not to follow it: therefore, over yourself I crown and mitre you." [1] Dante has retraced the steps of all humanity: he has returned from the *selva selvaggia*, the wild wood of error, to the ordered wood of primal innocency; and Virgil, whether he symbolizes Reason, or is the representative of Empire, is about to disappear, handing his office on to Beatrice, the symbol of theology. But before he goes we must note that he also has made his contribution to the Earthly Paradise: for Dante had seen the similarity of the Golden Age of Virgil and his fellow-poets, when the world was governed right, to the descriptions of Eden, and the two conceptions have coalesced to make the symbol of the right ordering of the active life in whose possibility he believes. Dante, as he moves forward timidly into the eternal springtime of the wood, sees 'a lady by herself go singing and choosing flower from flower from those with which was painted all her path.' [2] The flowers she picks are virtuous actions in the freedom of innocency, and as he gazes on the scene Dante blames the insolence of Eve which made us lose it.

I have spoken of illogicality, and I am not sure that it will have been so far gathered where it lies. It has its root in this: Dante's recipe for the world to go right consists, as we have seen, of a dual prescription—the Church to give the knowledge of truth, the Empire to provide the constraint which ensures the conservation of justice. But that remedy is Dante's faith, not anything that is, and we have seen he damns the world because it does not conform to either side of it. That view of the world, as being wrong, does not change as Dante moves towards beatitude: on the contrary, we shall find sterner denunciations of what he has left behind as he advances, and as the gap grows wider, and they will reach their climax with St. Peter's invective against his own successor, Boniface VIII, and Rome: ' "He who usurps my seat on earth, my seat, my seat, that in the presence of the Son of God is vacant, has made my burial-place a sewer of blood and stench. . ." [3] Nor, obviously, as the hopes Dante attached to the person of the Emperor Henry VII fade and vanish, will Dante's views on the political disorder of his time lose sting and bitterness. There is a recipe propounded, and without it the world can only go astray. But since the world is without it, it is astray;

[1] *Purg.* XXVII, 124–42. [2] *Purg.* XXVIII, 40–2. *Par.* XXVII, 22–6.

and since Dante has embarked on a voyage through the supernatural world there is no room here for the description of what
does anyhow not exist. The *Divine Comedy* is harnessed on the
one side to a political allegory; but there is perforce no place
within it where that side can come to a fruition. Order (and it
was my warning in beginning) lies behind us, because it is an
arrangement from which we have departed, not an achievement
to which we might advance. And even so, as Dante looks behind
him, in spite of his conviction of the sanctity of those twin estab-
lishments of Church and Empire, there is no moment to point
back to when both were together right and operative. That is
why he slips insensibly further back, as was suggested by the
Cretan statue, to the Earthly Paradise as the Age of Gold. But
strictly speaking, this cannot be the symbol of world order under
the supreme authorities, for, being before the Fall, this is no place
for them. Crowned and mitred over himself, Dante is outside
the jurisdiction of the Empire or the Church: for the Earthly
Paradise is not what should be, it is instead—and how infinitely
different a thing it is!—what should have been. And therefore
here the flowers which grow spontaneously, and which are
picked as virtuous actions—they need no definition, no statement
of their content or direction. If we were right in our environ-
ment, and right also in ourselves, would not our actions automatically be right? Of course. But what then would they be?
It is the very question Dante does not need to ask, however much
we may want to; because his hand holds all the trumps, and it is
of the nature of trumps to cancel the opposition, not to arrange
it. It is not Machiavelli, as in the old accusation against him, who
reduces the world to a machinery, it is Dante. For once the
order is right then there is nothing to add to it, for to add is also
to change. There must be no content to human action for fear
of creating the world of man (which will be by definition
wrong) instead of the world of God (which was by definition
right). That is something very different from Machiavelli's
conviction of expansion when the problem of liberty has been
solved: 'Then one sees riches multiply in greater number, both
those that come from cultivation, and those that come from arts.
For every man multiplies willingly in that thing, and seeks to
acquire those goods, which he thinks he can enjoy when
acquired. So that it follows that men vie in private and public

convenience, and one and the other come marvellously to increase.'[1] Such is the expanding rhythm of liberty for Machiavelli, nor did Florence spread her name abroad in hell for him. But what would be the purpose of such an element in Dante's thought? Instead, when Pope and Emperor are in accord, established each in his respective sphere, the world will fall into its order, by definition. But in the absence of that accord, as of the partners to it, there looms behind that hypothesis the other hypothesis of the Earthly Paradise, where neither Pope nor Emperor had place, and where man was free and virtuous in his own right. The irony is that the Earthly Paradise becomes for Dante, for want of another one, the symbol also of the right ordering of the active life. Yet it needs no ordering, and there is no other activity than the token one of picking flowers.

It is a reminder that the *Divine Comedy* must aim elsewhere than at the earth, and here is the root of Dante's innocent betrayal of one part of his ideal. You cannot pass upwards without losing interest in what you left below. I said that Dante would turn into a theory his ideas on the difference between earthly and spiritual goods: it is in the middle of *Purgatorio*: 'Since your desires go to things where part is lost through company, envy moves the bellows to your sighs. But if instead love for the highest sphere twisted your desires aloft, this fear would not be in your breast. For all the more who say there, This is ours, each one possesses so much more of good, and burns the more with charity in that sphere.'[2] Can things be divided, yet increase? If we ask that question, as Dante did, the answer that comes is that our difficulty of comprehension arises because we keep our mind only on earthly things. What is the conclusion of this argument? Is it not obviously, that we should transfer affection from things which are invidious by their nature? *Adhaesit pavimento anima mea*—my soul stuck to the ground. What remedy can there be to this, except detachment? At this point the trend of thought which had been Dante's own meets the orthodoxy of the Middle Ages, and bows to it. For it may be that earthly things are wrong in their arrangement; but it may equally be that they are wrong in their essence, because they are not infinity. Dante began with the first postulate: he made room for a temporal, as well as a spiritual, beatitude; and he made the active

---

[1] *Discorsi*, II, II, 199 (1813).   [2] *Purg.* XV, 49–57.

life the best for us because it was within our reach. But as he moves towards the spiritual realm the contemplative ideal reasserts itself, and kills the other one, though without Dante ever quite recognizing the conflict generated, or the effects of victory. But at the end of the scale there comes the exulting cry that Dante gives in paradise: 'O senseless cares of mortal men, how far defective are the syllogisms that make you flap your wings below! Some went after Law, some read the *Aphorisms*, some followed priesthood, some rule by force or trickery, some robbery, some civil occupations, some laboured, wrapped up in the pleasures of the flesh, some gave themselves to ease; whilst I, set free from all these things, with Beatrice was up in heaven so gloriously received!'[1] It is to be observed how all-embracing is this text: it is not the order which is wrong, and must be changed, it is the substance which is worthless, and had better be abandoned. By its context, it is the prelude to the canto of St. Francis, the spouse of Poverty; but it refuses to be limited to that context. It is the reaction of Dante (and he stands for man in general), not just the equation of St. Francis.

If we look back now, from paradise which we have anticipated for a moment, to purgatory, we shall see that this new attitude is developing there. The theory of Love admitted a natural, or instinctive sort, which could not but be right; yet the same canto which sets it forth ends with the statement that there is no felicity in earthly goods, and only two cantos have to pass before Dante has established that these are false in show, and deadly in effect. *Adhaesit pavimento anima mea*—the text I quoted earlier comes from this canto.[2] And later, when Dante meets Beatrice in the Earthly Paradise, she accuses him of not having followed her own passing by death from flesh to spirit by a similar conversion: ' "He turned his steps into a way that is not true, following false images of good which never keep their promise whole." '[3] And Dante, in the next canto, adds his confession to point her accusation: 'Weeping I said: "Scarcely was your face hidden from me than present things with their false pleasure turned my steps." '[4] False are the pleasures of the world, fallacious are the things around us. What is there to add? There is this only, that we are alive with a life which is a running down to death.[5]

It will be seen, I hope, that if my account of Dante's journey

---

[1] *Par.* XI, 1–12. [2] *Purg.* XIX, 73. [3] *Purg.* XXX, 130–2.
[4] *Purg.* XXXI, 34–6. [5] *ibid.*, 53–4.

has become involved in argument the difficulty was of Dante's making, rather than of my seeking. We might think of what he says as lying like a capital Y. The straight shaft is his constant view of his time (might we not have the same of ours?) as being turbulent and wrong. Then comes the fork: to the left lies the remedy for ridding the world of all its travail, and setting it in peace and quietude under Pope and Emperor. But the Emperor is missing, and the Pope is wrong, so Dante can only indicate the way, and it is to the right hand that there lies the way which Dante travels: it is the mystic ascent of purgatory and paradise. However great the will to do so, you cannot travel in two directions; and as Dante travels to the right it happens also that he discovers that there was no need to think of travelling to the left. Not only that there was no need, but that there were sirens and danger on the road. What should Dante do, but copy St. Bonaventure, who in great matters always put behind the left-hand care? One sets in order what one values, not what one throws away. We see now the full significance of that exultant cry: 'Whilst I, set free from all these things, with Beatrice was up in heaven so gloriously received!' The left-hand road has withered, without Dante ever acknowledging it. The earth is without order, the Earthly Paradise is a memory and a vision. But we are worms born to form the angelic butterfly. Why should we creep about? Cast out the ballast from the balloon, and it soars into the air until the earth looks small; and faster than this we shall find Dante and Beatrice in their return, upwards, not downwards.

We are free, now that we are sure in which direction we are going, to resume our examination of Dante's poem. Before I pass from *Purgatorio* there are some indications that I should add to those which concern its structure. The figures which stand out in relief are fewer than in *Inferno*, though we shall find a noble portrait of Sordello in Canto VI, Sordello who stands alone, proud and aloof, 'and in the moving of his eyes honest and slow. He did not speak a single word to us, but let us go, watching only like a lion in repose.'[1] But Virgil asks the way of him, and Sordello, instead of answering, asks where they were born. Virgil replies, '"Mantua . . .,"' loosing thereby the affection of Sordello, who is himself a Mantuan. And while Virgil and

[1] *Purg.* VI, 63–6.

Sordello embrace each other, Dante pours out his lament over the
strife in Italy, the faction which forms the contrast to this scene:
' "Oh, servile Italy, abode of grief, a ship without a pilot in the
storm, once mistress over provinces, and a brothel now! That
gentle soul was so quick, at the sweet name only of his town,
to welcome here his fellow-citizen; and now in you your living
ones are never without war, and one another gnaws of those
whom city walls and moat enclose." '[1]   The theme leads Dante
to an appeal to the Emperor Albert to take his place in the saddle
in Italy, and as well to the ironical apostrophe to Florence, rich,
peaceful and wise, so that the argument is not for her! It is the
irony of Dante's exasperated love for his birthplace. Or, after
Sordello, we may look to the episode of Statius, where Dante's
affectionate admiration for Virgil, chief of poets, is poured forth.
We have twisted our ideas of the poet's standing now another
way: poetry is for us something of an affectation, and the poet an
oddity. But Statius gives him different rank: ' "I had the name
that is most lasting and gives most honour," '[2] and all his worth
poetically he draws from Virgil. The words are those of Statius,
but the inspiring voice—in spite of the differences that we may
find between the poetic temperament of Dante and of Virgil—
is that of Dante; and no warmer tribute to the greatness of Virgil
has ever been paid.

I shall say little of the mystic procession in the Earthly Paradise
with its elaborate symbolism and intricate allegory to body forth
the history of man, his fall and his redemption, not forgetting
Dante's recipes for world-order. It is Dante's most ambitious,
and complicated, effort, fed from the most mystic pages of the
Old and New Testaments; and I shall venture to express my
sentiment that poetry and branching candlesticks are not synony-
mous. Once we have witnessed it, and once Beatrice has given
the final reassurance to Dante of the coming of the DUX who
shall set the world to rights, we shall be ready to take wing.
Dante who emerged to see the stars after the night of hell, is
ready now to rise to them. 'The glory of Him who moves all
things pierces the universe, and shines in one part more and in
another less. I went into the heaven which takes most of his light,
and saw things which one descending from up there cannot
recount.'[3] *Paradiso* opens with the statement of ineffability; and

[1] *Purg.* VI, 76–84.   [2] *Purg.* XXI, 85.   [3] *Par.* I, 1–6.

it proceeds with the warning that beatitude may be too much for us. 'O you who are in little boats, anxious to hear, following my ship that passes as I sing, go back and seek again your shores: put not out upon the sea, lest losing me perhaps you should be lost. The waters that I enter on were never sailed; Minerva breathes, Apollo leads me on, and the nine Muses point me out my course.'¹ That may give us pause. But it is right, nevertheless, that we should soar, and sandwiched in between those passages is the confirmation of what we saw developing as an attitude in purgatory, with its consequence. The epithet that we saw emerging for the world was that of *false*, and the first canto of *Paradiso* picks it up. As fire rises upwards by its nature, so does man towards the Empyrean. Yet at times we see the lightning striking downwards from the clouds, and so man can be warped as well 'if his first impetus is by false pleasure twisted to the earth.'² Dante himself has washed away all memory of his faults: the ballast has been thrown overboard, what can hinder further the upward flight? 'The concreate and perpetual thirst for the divine kingdom carried us up as fast almost as you can see the sky. Beatrice looked up, and I looked up to her.'³ We are leaving the earth behind us, without regret. Nor can the inhabitants of paradise speak differently. Boethius wrote a work which shows the world 'fallacious' to those who read it right, and he 'came out of martyrdom and exile to this peace.'⁴ Dante's own ancestor, Cacciaguida, who at the centre of this last canticle looks backward to a time when things were better in Italy (the backward glance to better times which we have seen in Canto XVI of *Inferno* and *Purgatorio*, to confirm our feeling that the world was slipping from what was right, not moving to it), Cacciaguida echoes significantly the formula of Boethius. Under the Emperor Conrad he fought, and died, in a crusade against the Saracen: 'There was I by that foul race set free from the fallacious world whose love fouls many souls; I came from martyrdom into this peace.'⁵ And what will Dante think when for a moment he looks down, instead of looking up? We shall find his statement at the end of Canto XXII when Beatrice turns his gaze from the final contemplation of the infinite to which he is approaching over the path he has traversed. What can the earth

¹ *Par.* II, 1–9. ² *Par.* I, 134–5. ³ *Par.* II, 19–21.
⁴ *Par.* X, 125–6; 129–30. ⁵ *Par.* XV, 145–8.

seem when one looks down on it from seven heavens' height?
'With my eyes I then went back through all the seven spheres,
and saw this globe such that I smiled at its puny air; and for the
best I take that counsel which makes the least of it; and he who
thinks of other things can truly be called just.'[1]

Dante at the outset of the *Comedy* damned Celestine V amongst
the pusillanimous because he made the 'great refusal,' because he
abjured the papacy to live a hermit.[2] And the Dante who passed
that judgment is himself traditionally proud and arrogant in his
character. We may remember the anecdote when Dante was
proposed ambassador to the Pope at Rome: 'If I go who remains?
If I remain who goes?' And human fame sometimes in his poem
is something to be striven for, in *the great desire for excellence*:[3]
for in our ears, as in those of many others, there may ring the
words of Virgil to Dante at a moment of lassitude in hell:
' "Henceforth you must bestir yourself," my master said, "for
lying in feathers or under quilts one does not come to fame, and
if you use your life up without fame you leave no other trace on
earth than smoke in air, or foam upon the wave." '[4] Those are
potent words. But we must balance them against the denial of
the use of fame which comes in purgatory. 'What is the rumour
of the world but wind, which blows now here, now there, and
changes name because it changes side? . . . Your reputation is
the colour of the grass, which comes and goes, and he discolours
it who brings it freshly from the ground.'[5] Surely, the grass of
springtime lasts no longer than the smoke, leaves no more traces
than the foam? How do we resolve this opposition? to which
do we give credence, the necessity, or the uselessness of Fame?
The final answer of Dante is from that infinite distance when he
looks down through seven spheres to see the world, and it is
small. It is only 'the little patch of earth that makes us all so
fierce,'[6]

l'aiuola che ci fa tanto feroci

and Dante is the first traveller to discover Lilliput. Dante himself
makes his refusal, and it is perhaps greater than Celestine's,
although it is not damned. As he turns with the constellation of
the Twins, 'the little patch of earth that makes us all so fierce
appeared to me whole, from the mountains to the river-mouths.

---

[1] *Par.* XXII, 133–8.   [2] *Inf.* III, 60.   [3] *Purg.* XI, 86–7.
[4] *Inf.* XXIV, 46–51.   [5] *Purg.* XI, 102–2; 115–17.   [6] *Par.* XXII, 151.

And then I turned my eyes towards her lovely eyes.' It is Beatrice, and beatitude, that matters, not the world.

We are back, and it will already have been realized, to that exulting cry of detachment from earthly things which is the prelude to Canto XI and to the exaltation of St. Francis and St. Dominic. These, for Dante, are the two wheels of the chariot of refuge for the Church, and as wheels must, they work in unison. ' "He was called Dominic, and I speak of him as of the husbandman whom Christ elected in his garden for his aid. Well did he seem the messenger and familiar of Christ, for the first love he showed was for the first counsel which Christ gave. And oftentimes his nurse found him silent and wakeful on the ground, as if to say: I came for this." '[1] And Francis too fell in love in his youth with one who does not normally attract. ' "She, losing her first husband, remained eleven hundred years and more, despised, obscure, without an offer till he came; nor was it of avail to hear that he who made the whole world tremble at his voice found her secure with Amiclas; nor was it of avail to be constant or obdurate, so that she, where Mary stayed below, went up with Christ upon the Cross. But so that I may not proceed obscurely, take henceforth Francis and Poverty as these lovers in my prolix speech. Their concord and their happiness made wondrous love and sweet looks be the cause of holy thoughts: so that the venerable Bernard unshod himself to run after such peace, and, running, thought himself still slow. Oh unknown riches, fruitful good! Aegidius casts his shoes away, Sylvester does so too, following the bridegroom, so pleasing was the bride." '[2] St. Dominic began as a baby on the bare ground: and finally it will be the bare ground in which St. Francis, dying, wishes burial, 'and for his corpse he wished no other bier.'[3]

Adhaesit pavimento anima mea, my soul stuck to the ground, and that adhesion to the earth was wrong. But this adhesion to the bare earth is a different one, and something meritorious. 'For it is right that he should end in endless grief who, for the love of things which do not last eternally, strips off this love.'[4] We must throw out the ballast of the temporal, in order to rise into the spiritual. Dante and Beatrice soar up through the nine

[1] *Par.* XII, 70–8.   [2] *Par.* XI, 64–84.   [3] *ibid.*, 117.
[4] *Par.* XV, 10–12.

heavens to the Empyrean. Light floods them, in the infinity of
space. Here sense-impressions are outranged, or are the paltry
substitutes for supra-sensual realities; and the way is of necessity
interspersed with Dante's admissions that his eye cannot see, or
else his tongue narrate. Even, for us, some of the grand conceptions which Dante imagined in the fourteenth century may
have tarnished a little in another world. In the galaxy of light
Dante sees the ladder of light up which, as moving lights, the souls
of the blessed flit along; or he sees them form themselves, from
separate lights, into the luminous apotheosis of the imperial sign,
the sacred Eagle, flashing through the sky. It was, doubtless, a
grand conception, this final magnification of the Empire in which
Dante still believed when he had cast the world away. But we
have seen the lights flit up and down, and luminous advertisement
against the sky; and in our disappointment with electric signs can
measure the inadequacy of human imagination penetrating the
unknown. Dante at times can express the confidence, and the
felicity, of beatitude: 'like the lark that first soars singing in the
air, and then is still, content with the last sweetness overfilling
her.'[1] It is his silence here which is more convincing than any
words could be; and we may find ourselves spying the places, in
between the dazzle and the distance, where Dante still looks back,
whether in sorrow, anger, or affection, to the details of the world
he knew. If *Paradiso* is tantalizing, it is not because Dante is the
wrong poet to attempt portraying it. It is because all men must
before its vision prove inadequate. *Paradiso* ends in the climax of
the contemplation of God, and Dante, with all his visual confidence, repeats eleven times in one canto the confession of un-
responsive faculties. What matters most is also least communicable; and Dante, who had seen so much, ends only with 'I think
I saw because I like to think.'[2] Lest that should appear a faint,
or a pessimistic, end, something to turn the reader back from
reaching it, or reading him, I wish to end this brief account of
Dante's journey with one of those brilliant passages, the one
where Dante bids us suspend our judgment in the individual
case, and offers hope for consummation out of misery: 'Let not
men be too sure in judgment, as one who thinks the corn ripe
in the field before it is; for I have seen the thorns the winter

[1] *Par.* XX, 73–5.   [2] *Par.* XXXIII, 91–3.

through seem fierce and hard, then bear the rose upon their tip; and once I saw a ship sail swift and straight over the sea through all its course, to sink at last at entry to the port. Let not Gammer This or Gaffer That, seeing one rob, another offering, think that they see them in God's mind: for one may rise, the other fall.'[1]

[1] *Par.* XIII, 130–42.

DANTE AND VIRGIL

DANTE AND VIRGIL

WE have passed rapidly over the ground covered by Dante's journey, and can turn towards this question of the comparison of a pair taken generally—since Dante did his best to make them so—as being inseparable. How does this poem of Dante stand in relation to the other poem of Virgil? Is Virgil willing to act as Dante's guide, or was he pressed into his service? Are they similar as poets? Which way do they look, what are they like? It is a subject on which we may derive, even without knowing it, prejudices from earlier criticism; and it is one on which we may also derive support from the same source. For these two reasons this is the moment to cast back our eye over the English interest in Dante, which we shall find, at its own level, not inarticulate on the relationship between the two. Then we shall see as well that some elucidation of the matter has been achieved later by other scholars than our own, although I think the theme of Dante and of Virgil is one still that is unexhausted, and virtually even, unattempted. But since the argument is an important one, it will be well to draw our breath, and gather up our information, before we exercise our judgment.

In the nineteenth century there was a succession of Englishmen who occupied themselves, at various levels, with Dante. Carlyle was the chief herald of our enthusiasm, placing Dante firmly among the demigods of poetry—he who, a century before, had been in a measure outside the list. Warren Lord Vernon built a monument to this new fame of Dante, the Poet as Hero, or the Hero as Poet. He set himself to amass a library of all the editions of Dante, and of all the works on Dante. And his own publications echoed that interest; while their format linked him with the noble patrons of literature of earlier time. His juxtaposition of the four earliest texts of the *Divina Commedia* pointed the way towards textual criticism. His stately edition of the *Inferno*, with its parallel setting out of the allegories according to the discrepant views of the corpus of commentators, its paraphrase of the text to ensure its comprehension, its list of Dante editions, its ensuing apparatus of illustration—this is the main monument of Lord Vernon. It is not so much an exegesis of Dante as a demonstration of its necessity and a base on which to work, something so strong and solid as to leave no doubt as to the magnitude of Dante, and of the problems to which his work gives rise.

Perhaps in between Lord Vernon and his true successors we should place on a mezzanine the Rossettis, with their resurrection of the *Early Italian Poets*, of the *Vita Nuova*, of *Dante and his Circle*, with the overflow into the Pre-Raphaelite school of illustration and the multiplication of the image (unattractive, and, I hope, inaccurate) of *Beata Beatrix*. Rossetti père had bent over the *Divine Comedy*, with results not over-valuable, but Rossetti children looked to the *Vita Nuova* and the *dolce stil novo*. They did not turn those introductory pages of Vernon's folio, with the *Prospects* of all the allegories, the hints of Dante's cosmogony, and the figures of his voyage. But while they pursued a path which kept Dante in the public eye, and linked him with a somewhat popular taste, so that all readers knew of him, at least as a symbol, there were others who took up the work which Vernon had only pointed out. It is not part of my intention here to map them out in detail: they are a preface to my argument, and not a main concern. Two names stand out amongst them, though not quite on the same level: Edward Moore, and Paget Toynbee. The first of these brought the wide reading and the apparatus necessary for the task: the establishment of Dante's text, his indebtedness to the main writers of antiquity (and it is here that we are waiting for him,) the charting of time-references in the *Divina Commedia*, which leads on in turn to the astronomy of Dante's world; and then he still had energy to overflow, as onto the earlier biographers of Dante. Indeed, we can get an idea of the appetite of Moore from a chance remark in the *Studies in Dante*: he said, too many readers fought shy of Dante's astronomical indications; they should study the Ptolemaic system, and would find what a lot they could understand; he himself hoped to write on it, and did. By the side of this close occupation with a vast field of necessary research Paget Toynbee's contribution seems less important, and a little dilettante: though may not this be merely the inevitable effect of following on in a field of research which has been opened up? The life of Dante has been often written, and rewritten; and Paget Toynbee's studies deal mostly with minor points. Perhaps, as a measure of the distance between leader and lieutenant of the Oxford Dante school, we should place Paget Toynbee's anthology of the beauties of Dante, *In the Footprints of Dante*, alongside Moore's *Studies in Dante*. It is Moore, after all, who is the editor of the Oxford Dante; and it is he one feels who gives the impetus to such later scholars as Wicksteed (*Dante and Aquinas*) and Edmund Gardner (*Dante and the Arthurian Legend*). By the side of his work Paget Toynbee's other long anthology, *Dante in English Literature*, reveals a different principle: it is rather a discursion from Dante than a collection of material for the understanding of him in his formation. Moore was concerned with what went into Dante: Toynbee primarily with what interest men had taken in him.

That is intentionally brief as an indication of an operosity which lasted, as did the English cult for Dante, until the first Great War. Naturally, the diminuendo of this movement continues after the barrier of the war, as notably with Edmund Gardner; but nevertheless, after that break no new recruit continues in England this labour of love and scholarship for Dante. After the effort for the centenary in 1921 the English stream of Dante publications drops till it is represented almost solely by the Temple Classics edition of the text; and this publication remained stationary, as it had been at the beginning of the century. How sharp the break is can be seen by the nature of the rare new work on Dante: Mr. Eliot, for a series called the *Poets on the Poets*, wrote an introduction in appreciation which is innocent of Dante-erudition, concerned as it is with the nature of the poetry; and perhaps it is not the most conclusive of Mr. Eliot's criticism. Mr. Charles Williams wrote, again without the apparatus, on the *Figure of Beatrice*, and in so doing was sufficiently *arriéré* to be able to mix his own mysticism with the nineteenth-century cult for the blessed damozel; so that he descends from the Rossettis rather than from Dr. Moore. Mr. C. R. Buxton, in *Prophets of Heaven and Hell*, put in his plea for Dante ('the most piercing of human intellects') and for the long poem to be read in its entirety. But it was Buxton's respect for the *Divine Comedy* —as for the other three prophetic works—which emerged from his booklet, rather than any piercing statement on the reasons for his respect; nor can we find in him any awareness of the problem which suggests itself to me of the relationship between Dante and Virgil. Rather, for Buxton, Milton and Goethe join the pair as being also in some mysterious way identical; though perhaps

Milton might be taken as being, by definition, the most un-dantesque of poets. None of these books, then, is in the tradition of Edward Moore and Paget Toynbee. They emphasize instead the fact of its disappearance. If Williams refers once to an authority, it is to one who is down the list and off the horizon, and no less revealing is Buxton's single supporting reference to such *vieux jeu* as Dean Church's *Essay on Dante*. If even those who still occupy themselves with Dante here do so with such per-functory looking to the *apparatus criticus* in its present, or in any, state, or at levels where there is no point in looking back, then it may be assumed that for the literary public generally, the labours of Moore, and their continuation in Dante criticism elsewhere, have no existence.

For the one half, this represents a change of tastes; for the other, a change of methods. The literary public for Dante no longer exists to the extent it did, and perhaps it is too late to recapture the fervour and respect for Dante which once made him as much an English province as Shakespeare was a German one; and Mr. Eliot, who still proclaims to a lessened company that Dante stands supreme among poets, is no longer occupied with erudi-tion. The formula of Moore was complication, its type *Dante and* . . . (as *Dante and the Vulgate, Dante and Astronomy*); the formula of Eliot is appreciation, his title *Dante*. And perhaps it is this particular which may embolden me to examine Dante *and* Virgil with a view to their essence, rather than with a view to the ways in which they combine. Partly, too, Dr. Moore dug his own pit: on the one side the *Oxford Dante*, a plain text of all the works; on the other, the *Studies in Dante* as gathering in his work around the text. The first is no longer authoritative. We do not call the *Convito* the *Convito*, but the *Convivio*. Multiply these little shifts, not only of course in the names of books, and you have removed usefulness from Moore's edition, which cannot now compete with any Italian one. And the second? They represent in reality a cross section, or a series of cross sections, of the annotations that can be made to Dante, and as such, where they were new and valuable, they have long since been incorporated into the modern Italian annotated editions of Dante. It was the vastness of the field then to be explored that had attracted Moore. 'They will, I hope, enable students to form a more complete idea than was before possible of the encyclopaedic character of Dante's learning and studies.' That is something perfectly distinct from the identity of Dante's poetic temperament, and it may seem that literature lays prudently in store authors whose work is large and complex, for the exercise of patient research and elucidation. It is akin to the task undertaken in the first thirty years of this century in the examination of Rabelais, who also had been hard to understand. It is something that required diligence rather than critical assessment, and it may end, as seems possible with the elucidation of Rabelais's thought, in the final confession that an author who had seemed to have everything to say had in reality much less than might have been supposed. Moore did not start, as did the Société des Etudes Rabelaisiennes, from the beginning: no one till him had covered *all* the works of Dante, but much had been done; and many experts at Oxford were ready round Dr. Moore for specialist consultation. That does not lessen his merit in the prodigious task he undertook, but it explains why his work does not still stand by itself. It was bound to fall back into the notes which impede the progress of the conscientious reader (you and I) of the *Divine Comedy*. It was a task, however vast and intricate, that could reach completion: had not Dante (it is matter for our admiration, says Dr. Moore) assembled 'this surprising amount of learning' in one lifetime, and without the aid of dictionaries, notes, concordances? Must not modern scholarship, furnished with all these aids, be capable of following him? And when the long task is completed, what is there left to do, but to applaud and then to go away? Assuredly, since the tide had receded from Dante himself, there was no likelihood of a new scholar in England, or a new brotherhood of scholars, beginning all again *daccapo*. Moore, and with him, though to a lesser extent, Paget Toynbee, punctuate the pages of the most recent Italian editions of Dante; and we may feel that their contribution to the elucidation of the author whom they so much revered was valuable and has been accepted, even though we have for the most part put their volumes decently upon one side.

But it is natural that I, puzzled by Dante's lines at the beginning of the *Comedy*, ' "You are my master and my author; you alone are he from whom I took the style has brought me honour," '

"tu se'solo colui da cui io tolsi
lo bello stilo che m'ha fatto onore,"

wondering what Dante had by then written among his sonnets and *canzoni*, in the prose of the *Vita Nuova* or of the treatises, that he could label as Virgilian, wondering if Dante ever was Virgilian, should turn back first to Dr. Moore's studies, and in especial to the section headed *Dante and Virgil*. In spite, however, of the heading I do not find that the question had occurred to Moore. The admiration for the quantity of Dante's learning is, as we suspected, inimical to the assessment of Dante's quiddity, either in itself, or in relation to another poet. The labour of elucidation is of the back, more than of the brain; and the reverence is of a different sort from that which produced earlier the counsel,

> Nulla dies tamen interea, tibi nulla abeat nox,
> Quin aliquid vatum sacrorum e fontibus almis
> Hauseris, ac dulcem labris admoveris amnem.

That is an invitation to read poetry as something that belongs peculiarly to us. But Moore is busy listing parallels, and may even miss the import of what himself establishes. For instance, in this catalogue of Dante's echoes, Moore remarks that Dante was saturated with certain authors, especially with the Scriptures and with Virgil. He notes the frequent repetition of small phrases and Virgilian epithets, and adds that familiarity with the original on the part of his readers was assumed by Dante. Yes; but then, this saturation with at least the matter of Virgil is of Dante's time, something which does not define the individual Dante any more than it defines his background? In the same way, the method of cataloguing is good for some overall tests, but not for all. It may be easy to appear Virgilian at the moment where one is imitating Virgil, and a collection of such imitative passages (which obviously is the substance of Moore's section) might have some uniformity of texture. But another test would be to see if Dante is usually Virgilian in method or in quality in the places where he is not derivative from Virgil. And there is, of course, no room for such a line of research in the *Studies in Dante*. Not that Moore omitted a caveat, but it is to be found elsewhere, and there is no record of his having drawn a conclusion from it. 'We are surprised at his enthusiastic, and, as it appears to us, somewhat extravagant admiration of (Statius) whose prolix and often inflated style is the very antipodes of his own.' Admiration, and quotation, then, is not by way of being a certificate of resemblance. And if it is possible to admire Statius, and yet remain at the antipodes to him, might it not be possible also to admire Virgil even more, to speak of him the affectionate words that we have seen put into the mouths of Statius and Sordello, and yet remain essentially unlike him?

Such is the inquiry that presents itself. But if it is very different from that of Moore it is plain that in pursuing it we need not disdain as a preliminary his information, or that of those who have (in other countries) followed after him. Otherwise we might find ourselves beset by the same dangers as Buxton or Charles Williams. Firstly, we may note that some have ventured to place Dante's admiration for Virgil even higher than Moore knew. The latter noticed the order of Dante's quotation of the poets in the *Vita Nuova* as Virgil, Lucan, Horace, Homer, Ovid (though this does not really constitute an order of merit), but he envisaged Homer as being set over Virgil in the placing of *Inferno* IV. But does Virgil necessarily slip into second place among these others whom he enumerates himself? Other critics have seen in Dante's comment, 'So did I see together met the school of that master of the highest song, who soars like eagle over all the rest,' an indication of Virgil, not of Homer, as the supreme poet: does not the *altissimo* of this passage echo the other *altissimo* a dozen lines before in that stirring line,

"Onorate l'altissimo poeta,"

'Honour the most high poet,' and he is Virgil. If that does not clinch the point, yet to all practical purposes it equates the two in merit; and, since Dante does not know Homer, it is Virgil who must be for him the height of poetry experienced. But there is too here the eagle, that *sacrosanto segno*, and what is it doing if it is not linked with Virgil, who is Dante's chosen guide because he is the singer of the Empire, because of the parallel between the Eagle and the Cross, between Aeneas and his contemporary David? It is (and this is a point Moore knew) the absence of the Empire in 1300 that throws an obstacle between all men and the right-ordered active life. That is why, in an age saturated in some manner with Virgil, Dante says that his great love is the cause ' "that made me seek your volume out," '

"che m'ha fatto cercar lo tuo volume."

It was not Virgil's poem that he had had to seek out, for that was
known well enough; but the acceptance of his political message
as Dante read it. That is a difference which may well falsify in
its reaction Dante's view of Virgil. And it is because the Empire
had been in abeyance for so long that Virgil, on his first appearance, was as one 'who seemed weak through lengthy silence.'
Did not Dante hold that the Empire was lapsed since at least the
death of Frederick II in 1250? Such an interregnum of political
silence was enough to cause some hoarseness in the Empire's
representative! And this interpretation of the puzzling passages
of *Inferno* I may also serve to show the advance in skill since the
days of honest John Boccace and his dilation on dryness or vis-
cosity—for either of these opposites might equally be the cause—
in the passage from the lungs which hampered speech *infintan-
toché o rasciutta o sputata non è*.

Interesting also is the advance in insight into Dante's reasons
for altering the Virgilian account of Mantua's origin. 'Why he
did so, or what other authority he was following, I am unable to
say,' wrote Moore, though he was quite right in seeing instinctively the words put in Virgil's mouth as a sort of 'retractation.'
Dante insists upon the separation of Virgil from the charge of
magic, which still plays round him nonetheless in the commentary which Boccaccio made, so strong had been the legend of
the Middle Ages, and he epitomizes this acquittal in his account of
Mantua. Mantua got nothing from the soothsayer Manto but its
name, and this he emphasizes by the double contradiction of
what Virgil himself had put forward in the *Aeneid*: Manto
founded the city, not her son Ocnus; she is a virgin, and therefore
had no son Ocnus. Thus she left for the city Mantua no heredity
but her bones, and these also were inoperative: ' "she lived, and left
her empty body there. The men who had been scattered round
about drew later to that place, for it was strong by reason of the
marsh about it on all sides. They made their city over those dead
bones; because of her who chose the place before they called it
Mantua, drawing no other lots." '[1] Every detail there is eloquent
of Dante's intention to clear his guide of the taint which clung to
his reputation in the Middle Ages: Manto's connection with
the city Mantua is reduced to casualness, her body was an empty
one, men happened to be round and found the marsh-encircled

[1] *Inf.* XX, 87–93.

spot a stronghold, so that they built over those dead and un-communicative bones; and as a final safeguard from Manto, they built and named their city without any rites of divination. This effort to make a scission between Virgil and his legend is eloquent of Dante's estimate for his guide—the main place, perhaps, where he departs resolutely from the common traditions of his time, so high is the task before them both. Even more, this canto links with the succeeding one. In the first there is this strong affirmation of the innocence and the merit of Virgil. The *Aeneid*, to give it full relief above this bad charge of magic, is asserted as 'l'alta mia tragedía'[1]; and this praise is echoed at the beginning of canto XXI for the new sister-poem, 'So we came from bridge to bridge, talking of other things, ones which my comedy does not care to sing.'[2] 'L'alta mia tragedía,' says Virgil; 'la mia commedía,' answers Dante. They are linked, but are they not also differentiated by this statement? Meanwhile, secure in their consciences, and in the value of their poems, what should they be talking of, but of the calumny against them both? Canto XXI belongs to the barators, and baratry was the charge made by his political opponents against Dante. He is as anxious to dissociate himself from that as he had been to absolve Virgil from the charge of magic; and the colours of Canto XXI show the infinite distance to which he thrusts these barators beneath him.

Other details have been noticed since the time of Moore. There is at the outset a subtle gradation of tone, while Dante hovers on the verge of pusillanimity. Who are those that have made the descent to Hell? ' "You say that Silvius's father, in mortal body still, went into the immortal world, and with his senses knew it. . . . There went there then the Chosen Vessel, to bring back comfort for that faith which is beginning of salvation's way." ' The second instance partakes of the certainty belonging to the Scriptures: there is no shadow of doubt in the *Andovvi* which announces the departure of St. Paul. But Virgil is a pagan poet, from the time of false and lying gods, and his statements do not bear the imprint of any infallibility. Does not the *Tu dici* carry some suggestion of the frivolity of pagan utterance? and extend it back as well to the proposition of Virgil? 'I began: "Poet, and guide . . ." ' The pagan poets, to whose ranks Virgil belongs (and, as is known, Dante kept the term *poet*

[1] *Inf.* XX, 113.   [2] *Inf.* XXI, 1–3.

for antiquity alone, at least until, in *Paradiso* XXV, he felt certain of his own equality of stature, and used it for himself—a vernacular poet being only a *dicitore per rima*, or a *trovatore*) are authors of fables. Is it not this reflection which sets Dante wondering whether Virgil was right in offering to take him down into the supernatural world?

Of the same sort as this is the observation that has been made of a characteristic in Virgil's behaviour. Dante, as Moore pointed out, took much of the apparatus of hell from Virgil, especially from *Aeneid* VI: though we must be careful to remember that the use of mythological creatures like Charon and his compeers is not a sign of an awakened classicism in Dante, but a legacy of the Middle Ages. When the sense of Virgil's poetry had disappeared, these figures still were apprehensible. They had been accepted in the ecclesiastical writers, from St. Augustine and Lactantius downwards; hence also such transformation as they receive. Not all, of course, could remain as Virgil had imagined it: is not Lethe, for Dante, on the summit of Mount Purgatory? And many other details differ also. In these circumstances it is only human for Virgil-guide to be pleased when everything, or something, is as he had depicted it; and to expect his pupil Dante to recognize without being told what he had read often in the *Aeneid*. Thus in *Inferno* III, 70–8 all is as it was in the *Aeneid*. Yet Dante remains puzzled, and Virgil speaks to him with what looks like merely crossness. The early commentators looked for an explanation to Virgil's rather curt refusal of information, and found it hard to put one. Benvenuto said offhand that it was because the beginning needed silence and meditation. But that has not seemed adequate to more modern commentators, and it has seemed more reasonable to assume a peccadillo on the part of Virgil (one of those human touches, as with Beatrice, which save him from being a symbol only), and a corresponding pique here since his pupil has neither exclaimed nor recognized what he himself had nevertheless described so accurately.

There is another point that has been noticed in the relationship between Dante and Virgil which has its bearing on their respective conceptions of the nature of poetry. In *Inferno* XXX Dante listens intently to the vulgar brawl between Sinon and Maestro Adamo, when suddenly he finds, to his amazement, that for so

doing Virgil is on the point of quarrelling with him: 'I was
wholly caught in listening to them, when my master said to me:
"Look you now! almost I brawl with you myself." And when I
heard him speak to me with wrath . . .'

> Ad ascoltarli er'io del tutto fisso,
> quando'l maestro mi disse: "Or pur mira!
> che per poco che teco non mi risso."
> Quando'io'l senti' a me parlar con ira . . .[1]

This last line is one of the examples of Dante's skill in reproducing
in his verse the movements of the situation. Punctuate it with
three exclamation marks,

> Quand'io'l senti'! a me! parlar con ira!

to get the full flavour of Dante's rude awakening. But why
should Virgil quarrel with Dante at this point? It is not here,
as it often is, a question of time wasted and the need to press
forward on one's way, but of a divergence of opinion: 'for wish-
ing to hear that is a low wish,"

> "ché voler ciò udire è bassa voglia."[2]

Virgil, it has been observed, has no connection with Terence and
Plautus. He sings no vulgar people or things: he is the poet of
decorum, and he exalts even the humble. Was not the palm
given to him in eighteenth-century Europe over Homer, at least
in the description of the Cyclops, because he has no trivialities?
And Sinon himself, who figures here in this canto of Dante's,
where he gets only ridicule and scorn in a low and comic brawl
with the hydropic Maestro Adamo, had quite different treatment
in the *Aeneid*. Virgil-poet took Sinon seriously, as an instrument
almost of Rome's high destiny:

> Tantae molis erat romanam condere gentem. (I, 33)

'so great a business was the founding of the Roman race!' And
even apart from that high theme, if anything in the *Aeneid* is
apart from it, Virgil does not accept the trivial as stuff for poetry.
Dante's attitude is different, even in *Paradiso*, as witness the
degeneracy of the Franciscans,

> sí ch'è la muffa dov'era la gromma,

[1] *Inf.* XXX, 130–3. [2] *ibid.*, 148.

'so that there's mildew where the tartar was,'[1] which we may call already a dantesque, and a non-virgilian, line. And, naturally, Dante is always ready to use the trivial to characterize, as for instance in the low signal emitted by Barbariccia at the end of *Inferno* XXI. Ruskin, the *preux chevalier*, remarked on this latter flagrant case that the slightest trace of obscenity in any individual was a 'great and infallible sign of the lack of moral strength'; and that Dante had printed this failing admirably in all his portraits of the devils. That is, perhaps, rather a prim Victorian comment; but at least it may serve as a reminder of a genuine point of divergence between Dante and Virgil, one that seems recognized implicitly by Dante himself in this quarrel episode.

So we are brought back, from this consideration of the two travellers, Virgil and Dante, in the poem to the question of the nature of their individual poetry. Leaving aside Homer, whom Dante could not read, Virgil is the height of poetry for Dante, and Dante claimed absorption of Virgil's style. Now it is not irrelevant that Dante's view of Virgil is coloured throughout by theoretical considerations which belong to his own time, and have therefore no sure base in Virgil himself. Moore had noted that Dante considered the people of Rome as much God's chosen people as the Hebrews; and that he had quoted the *divinus poeta noster* at times as though he had all the authority of Scripture. The full reasons for that attitude have been brought out since Moore's time. It is not, once more, a foretaste of humanism, or a new classical interest; it is strictly related to Dante's theological preoccupations. Of the two views on the Fall Dante adheres to the less depressing one, which saw man bereft of his supernatural advantages, not of his natural ones as well. Man was not left in a state of complete impotence. He could use his natural faculties to order his life in this world. And after centuries human reason advanced to the height of this conception of Universal Empire, which for Dante represented its summit, and which was (since it was half the programme for that felicity of mankind envisaged in the *De Monarchia*) the necessary prerequisite for the Redemption. When man had done all that he could by himself, then was the moment for God to intervene and give due sanction to the Roman Empire. That is why those parallels which we have seen between Church and Empire all

[1] *Par.* XII, 114.

become so important for Dante. That is why Virgil, not
Aristotle, emerges in Dante's mind as the symbol—at first sight,
surely, a puzzling one—of Human Reason: because he is the
singer of Universal Empire, not merely because he had had
experience in travelling in hell. It is probably the reason also
why Dante does not think of 'saving' Virgil. Partly, Dante, as
usual with him, was content here to follow medieval traditions;
but also, how could Virgil remain as the representative of Human
Reason by itself before the Redemption if at the same time
Dante made him participant in the latter? Statius, and this
again is something without a sure base in the man himself, is the
trait d'union between Imperial and Christian Rome; and it is
when he comes to Statius that Dante, as well as emphasizing his
affectionate regard for Virgil, can emphasize too the lead which
in the medieval view Virgil had given towards Christianity—
Virgil, the author of the Fourth Eclogue. ' "You did like
him who goes by night, who bears the light behind him with no
profit for himself, but after him he makes the people see . . .
Through you I was a poet, and a Christian, through you." '[1]

> "Facesti come quei che va di notte,
> che porta il lume retro e sé non giova,
> ma dopo sé fa le persone dotte . . .
> . . . Per te poeta fui, per te cristiano."

Again Dante can accept the medieval tradition: Virgil remains in
Limbo, but Statius has been saved. And Virgil at least can lead
them both to the Earthly Paradise, which as we know is Dante's
symbol of this world ordered aright when reason and revelation
are combined.

Before we are left finally with the question of poetic identity
we have still some aid to receive from Dr. Moore. If we turn
back now to the sort of information which his statistics can give
us we shall find that out of some 1,500 passages in Dante's works
which by then had been discovered to be either quotations,
imitations or allusions to classical writers and to Scripture
Virgil claims only the third place. First is the Vulgate, with 500;
then comes Aristotle with 300; and after him Virgil, with 200.
And if we analyse for ourselves this latter figure, which Moore
only presented, we find that 90 of these passages concern the

---

[1] *Purg.* XXII, 67–9, 73.

Inferno, 34 the *Purgatorio*, and 13 the *Paradiso*, while the rest are scattered in Dante's other writings. When we remember that many of the imitations in the *Inferno* arise from the apparatus of the underworld, from material particulars rather than from the spirit, it is plain that the Virgilian qualities of Dante are limited, unless he is like Virgil where he has not imitated him. Nor must we forget that Moore excluded from his list such writers as the Fathers of the Church and the theologians. If we added a check-list for St. Thomas Aquinas we should be likely to find an inverse progression, and figures that are in all probability substantially higher. Nor would it be at all improper to say that Dante's poetic style often bears the imprint of Aquinas. And if, on the other hand, we analyse the figures from the *Aeneid* we shall see that Moore noticed 147 passages from the first six books, including 72, or roughly half, from Book VI itself, against 35 from Books VII–XII. So that there is something of a symmetrical pattern. Dante's interest in Virgil dwindles after the first half of the *Aeneid*, that is, in the books that are concerned with battle; and Virgil has a dwindling part in the *Divine Comedy* as Dante progresses towards theology. That pattern is not without its interest and its significance. Naturally, these figures are not absolutely exact. They include very vague, as well as very precise, reminiscences; and Moore may well not have been exhaustive. In fact, one omission in Moore shows the difficulty of this listening-in to echoes, even with all the help available from all one's fellow-commentators to Dante. Moore expressed surprise that, in spite of his mention of *Orazio satiro*, Dante 'never shows the slightest acquaintance with the *Satires*' (of Horace). But he had overlooked the fact that it was Horace who anticipated Dante in the image of the wood, and of the straight path lost.

> Velut sylvis, ubi passim
> Palantes error certo de tramite pellit,
> Ile sinistrorsum, hic dextrorsum abit: unus utique
> Error; sed variis illudit partibus.
>
> mi ritrovai per una selva oscura,
> ché la diritta via era smarrita.[1]

Is not that sufficiently precise to deserve, at least, to be the connection which determines the epithet of *Inferno* IV? But although

---

[1] Horace, *Sat.* II, iii; *Inf.* I, 2–3.

there may be rectifications to these tables of figures, and though I feel that they minimize, perhaps, the rôle of Ovid as a purveyor of material, I think that in their broad outlines they are near enough the truth; and in this 'incredible diligence' of the Middle Ages it is plain that the figures for Virgil do not stand for a great deal. The *Aeneid* has some 10,000 lines, and Dante's poem is almost half as long again. Two hundred passages—in one whose pattern is encyclopaedic—cannot by themselves affect the texture of Dante's poetry.

Nor, of course, can we here object the continual presence of Virgil-guide. Macrobius may have mentioned the old conception of the erudition of Virgil: 'He never makes a mistake in matters of learning.' He meant, he knew all about the auguries, for instance. But that is something quite different from the *famoso saggio*, the *mar di tutto il senno* of Dante's poem. The latter's erudition may be as likely as not on theological matters, and on the Christian ordering of hell. He has so much an identity of his own, belonging to the *Commedia*, and divorced from the *Aeneid*, that if we were to forget Dante's initial theories on the Empire, and then to change the name of the guide to something else than Virgil, and with this change of guide cancel a handful of obvious echoes of the *Aeneid*, we might (could we but start afresh our reading of the *Comedy*) read through without Virgil coming to our mind at all. Virgil-guide is the creature of Dante's imagination, as of Dante's misconceptions with regard to the place of Virgil's poem in the sequence of events leading to the Redemption, and the Revelation. That is part of the same shift by which Aeneas's descent to Hades becomes a journey to hear the causes of his victory, and to find amongst its consequences the *papal mantle* also. If Dante had approached the *Aeneid* with aesthetic preoccupations, and not with those of his own ideology, might we not have expected him to make more use of the poetical episode of Dido? Dido fills a whole book in Virgil's poem, and she is a presence in much more than that. It would be astonishing if Dante did not avail himself of Dido, and, indeed, he finds a place for her, and furthermore makes Paolo and Francesca belong to Dido's company: 'so from the throng where Dido is they came to us,'

cotali uscir de la schiera ov'è Dido.

But nobody could take Virgil as his guide, for whatever reason, and not name Dido somewhere; and the significant fact is the different use Dante has for Paolo and Francesca, who are the central figures of the canvas on the fringe of which Dido still lingers. They have their own importance in Dante's scheme: where civil order under the Emperor is lacking the best qualities go astray. Francesca speaks of *peace* for Dante, and of the river Po which finds its *peace* within the sea; and emphasizes by her repetition of the word the absence of the thing itself in the squally circle of the Lustful. That is another preoccupation than Virgil's was with Dido. Virgil includes Dido primarily so that he may motivate the unrelenting enmity between Rome and Carthage—hence the supreme importance of this episode. It is big with consequences (as in Dido's great invective), while Francesca's tragedy is itself merely a consequence. Dido has a human value which is magnified immeasurably because it dominates an avenue in the future: the greater she, who carries the destiny of a race within her. But Francesca has behind her, in the wrongness of the world's order, the causes of her undoing. The account is closed, not opened up, and in such circumstances she cannot rival Dido's stature.

Perhaps it is important here to speak against the theory that in the episode of Dido Virgil demonstrates the virtue of Aeneas, who would thus accomplish here his duty at the expense of his pleasure. It is a thesis which has been put forward in what we might call, without wronging it, a modern counterpart to Dante's views on Virgil, and with the idea that the transition from primitive to secondary epic is marked by a new sense of duty, which is in its turn on its way to Christianity. So that Virgil would become again, only legitimately, as pre-Christian as he once was wrongly thought in his rôle as author of the Fourth Eclogue. But this diminution of the stature of Dido cannot be upheld, nor is there stated any moral conflict in the mind of Aeneas when he leaves her. Aeneas and Dido are free and equal while they are together; and they are still free and equal when they part. Nor does Aeneas leave her for his duty, but for his kingdom. The sense of the *Aeneid* is not duty, but achievement, and pride in achievement, magnified to be an apotheosis. Dido, in such a scheme, can have no subordinate station: she represents, not pleasure failing before duty, but counter-achievement rivalling achievement, Hannibal against Scipio, Carthage against Rome. In no other way could she loom so large. And we may take her as typical of Virgil's poetic manner. Virgil, said Sainte-Beuve in a happy moment which abandoned any nicety of chronology, 'est le premier des poètes raciniens.' That is not only a warning incidentally to those who see Racine's qualities as Greek (because he read Euripides)—though once more, as for Virgil himself (who also, I imagine, read the Greeks) and as for Dante, so for Racine, what one eats becomes oneself, not vice-versa; it is an invitation also, if we like, to think of Dido as akin in treatment to Phèdre:

> Reginam petit. Haec oculis, haec pectore toto
> Haeret et interdum gremio fovet inscia Dido. (I, 717–8)

> C'est Vénus tout entière à sa proie attachée.

This is a procedure which we can best perhaps define by the misconception of its nature on the part of orthodox French criticism. 'Sous les noms héroïques, à travers les infortunes et les crimes extraordinaires, c'est la simple, générale, humaine vérité que Racine veut montrer.' Or we can see it even better with someone less wary than Lanson, as with the critic who saw in *Bérénice* nothing but a *mariage manqué*, with a nice young man who is only *modérément épris*. For that has accepted M. Lanson's invitation to look for average human conditions, but has destroyed the play, which from being a tragedy would then fall apart in mere indifference. Indeed, it is only if the theme of Titus's love for Bérénice is of maximum importance that it can balance in his mind against something else which also is of maximum importance, the ruling of the Roman world. And that is the burden of Bérénice's own explicit comment at the end,

> Adieu. Servons tous trois d'exemple à l'univers
> De l'amour la plus tendre et la plus malheureuse.

Nor was it for nothing that she herself gave earlier on her testimony that Titus was not our next-door neighbour:

> Parle: peut-on le voir sans penser comme moi
> Qu'en quelque obscurité que le sort l'eût fait naître,
> Le monde en le voyant eût reconnu son maître?

For Titus must stand opposite Bérénice as Aeneas opposite Dido: you cannot lessen either partner of either pair without diminishing by just so much the weight of the tragedy in which they are involved. It is by writing them up above the human level, not by writing them down that the poet has proceeded. The critics were, perhaps, only slightly wrong: but it is the wrongness which consists in looking through the opposite end of the telescope. Neither Virgil nor Racine begins (as say Corneille) with a distortion of human truths; but they proceed to weight and emphasis by a process of concentration and magnification which makes any comparison with average cases seem ridiculous. 'Ne sont-ce pas les éternelles tragédies de la vie réelle, les sujets toujours les mêmes que les journaux et les tribunaux offrent à notre sensibilité avide de se dépenser?' Phèdre and Dido, then, on a par with Mrs. Smith we read of in the *faits divers* last week? That is a strange negation of something immediately perceptible to the apprehension. There are no Didos in the world around us: that is why we turn to literature to find them. Phèdre and Dido are your true *senhal*.

> O quam te memorem virgo namque haut tibi vultus
> Mortalis nec vox hominem sonat.   (I, 327)

It is not only Venus who walks the earth as goddess,

> Et vera incessu patuit dea,   (I, 405)

nor is this a figure which bears any relation to the procedure of the *dolce stil novo*:

> Ella si va, sentendosi laudare,
> benignamente d'umiltà vestuta;
> e par che sia una cosa venuta
> da cielo in terra a miracol mostrare.[1]

The Virgilian formula is plenitude, not rarefaction.

And Dante in the *Comedy*, who after all has more means at his command than the ethereal poet of the *Vita Nuova*? There are plain reasons why the formula of Virgil or of Racine was not open to Dante, even had he apprehended it. Where he is free to take most from Virgil, in the *Inferno*, his hands are tied. You cannot detach Francesca in her own right and raise her to the magnitude of Dido, because she remains, however poignant her tragedy, subordinate to a theme. The great figures of the *Inferno*, Farinata, Capaneo, Jason, Ulysses . . . are rebels to Dante's God.

---

[1] *Vita Nuova*, XXVI.

The very swelling of their pride is weakness. The only mega-phone that could be behind them (as Venus behind Phèdre or Dido, as Jupiter behind Aeneas) is Lucifer; and Dante cannot use him so, for the very conclusive reason which we have already seen, that Lucifer himself has been reduced in Dante's handling to a mere anti-Trinity, devoid of all intelligence, freezing life, not enthusing it. Any one of these figures may dominate a canto; but none, not even Boniface, can resound throughout a canticle. Nor does Purgatory, with its cleansing from the *habitus peccandi*, the inclination that remains over from transgression, lend itself to a Virgilian treatment. It fits more with the softening outlines of Pia de'Tolomei (*Purg.* V, 130–6) than with either Dido or Francesca. Manfred can be no Titus, the master of the world. And Paradise is likely to be still less Virgilian, since here there can be no affirmation of personality that is not subordinated to the flood of light. Dante's poetic method (considered, at least, from this one point of view), instead of being the same as Virgil's, swings automatically to being its opposite.

And, indeed, not only in spite of Dante's acceptation of the political meaning of the *Aeneid*, but precisely because of it, Dante stands at opposite poles to Virgil. Virgil sees the temple of Janus closed, the whole world at peace, and to remain at peace. Out of his satisfaction at that vast achievement springs his poem. And so much is Virgil the poet of mildness and of peace that he falls short of his own level in the books of the *Aeneid* which deal with the conflict and the obstacles, with the detail of battle. After Book VIII—the most Roman, it has been said, of the books of the *Aeneid*—we look for Virgil's poetry in snatches; and find it in the pity which death arouses much more than in the joy of combat:

> Qualem virgineo demessum pollice florem,
> Seu mollis violae seu languentis hyacinthi,
> Cui neque fulgor adhuc nec dum sua forma recessit;
> Non jam mater alit tellus virisque ministrat.   (XI, 68)

It is, as has always been noted, that indefinable tremor of Virgil's emotion which is one of his chief hall-marks:

> Sunt lacrimae rerum et mentem mortalia tangunt. (I, 462)

That is not all Virgil, by any means: but it is an essential part of him because he lives in a world in which, however much may be

right, much also will be wrong. Aeneas may achieve his end, but
there will always be some Creusa, some Dido, or some Pallas to
have fallen by the way. His pity, therefore, will be always called
upon. But Dante lives in a world in which everything may be
wrong, but that is only because it is not what it ought to be,
because it is not right. In these conditions what is wrong calls up
indignation, more than it calls up pity. And pity dwindles till it
dies. 'Here pity lives by being wholly dead: who is more
criminal than he who brings his passions to God's judgment?'[1]
Pity is not absent when Dante begins his pilgrimage, but it
vanishes as he proceeds, and as he acquiesces in divine retribution.
And we have only to think back once again to that savage out-
burst of St. Peter against Boniface VIII to realize that indignation
is Dante's hall-mark, as pity is that of Virgil.

And this opposite is reflected in Dante's subject. After all,
the whole of Dante's world partakes not a little of the individual
tragedy of Dido who mourns alone at home, and herself absent
sees and hears an absent Aeneas:

> Sola domo maeret vacua stratisque relictis
> Incubat. Illum absens absentem auditque videtque. (IV, 82)

As Dido for Aeneas, so Dante for the Universal Emperor. He
applauds the Empire, and he takes its singer as his guide, only
because it is absent from the world he knows. Virgil and Dante
converge on the same point, but from opposite sides: which
means equally, therefore, that they diverge from that point also.
Instead of a fulness of contentment with the state of the world,
leading to the apotheosis of the whole process that has preceded it
(and on both sides, for the greater the obstacles, the greater also
the triumph over them; so that Dido swells with Aeneas), here we
have a maximum of discontent. Dante's Augustus can only be
glimpsed occasionally as the Veltro and the Dux of prophecy.
It is precisely for the reasons which make Dante choose Virgil
as his guide that he will be found not to resemble Virgil. And we
must remember in this context still that Dante, who is a medieval,
rejects the Middle Ages in the name of the great medieval ideals
(of Empire and of Papacy), because he finds them unfulfilled:
absent, or warped from their true function. Those twin ideals, so
often appealed to as universals dominating the medieval scene,
were not, of course, so in the sense that they represented effective

---

[1] *Inf.* XX, 28–30.

realities. It is because there was a lack of well-defined local, or national, entities that they were looked to so much: just as hills, though small or distant, stand out across an indistinguishing plain. Does not Dante hate Philippe le Bel, who stands for the emergence of national power in France, as much as Boniface? Does he not, and we shall return to it soon, hate in Florence its becoming an independent state?

This difference in outlook, in spite of the many places where Dante imitates Virgil, is all-pervasive. And here again we may do well to remember Racine. He had a formula in the preface to *Bajazet*: 'Les personnages tragiques doivent être regardés d'un autre oeil que nous ne regardons d'ordinaire les personnages que nous avons vus de si près.' And we may recall, in consequence of that, the treatment of the death of Hippolytus in the *récit de Théramène*: Hippolytus, dragged by his frightened horses across the stony ground, until his shapeless body is one wound. Yet there is no detail to impose this on our eyes, and for the simplest of reasons. We are not really meant to see it:

> Ce qu'on ne doit point voir, qu'un récit nous l'expose.

There are no ignoble details, for the same reason that there is no ignoble language: because they would not be consonant with a noble impression. I have quoted Racine, and I may equally quote Virgil. For Aeneas in his descent to Hades meets Deiphobus, and finds him cruelly mutilated in his ears and nose. But it is not the detail, though it is given, which receives the emphasis. It is the pity which his plight evokes, the cruelty of his unmerited fate.

> Atque hic Priamiden laniatum corpore toto
> Deiphobum vidit, lacerum crudeliter ora,
> Ora manusque ambas, populataque tempora raptis
> Auribus, et truncas inhonesto volnere naris.   (VI, 493)

It is *crudeliter* and *inhonesto* that echo from this description in our minds: not the details, but the pity and the wrongness of them. But the procedure of Dante is a different one. We saw the law of retribution, the *contrappasso* which governs the occupants of hell. Let us look at it for a moment in one of the most terrible of instances. Mahomet is one of the impressive dantesque figures of *Inferno*. It matters little that Dante's information on him is quite wrong. He thought of him (with that medieval ignorance of the east) as a disappointed cardinal who had founded heresy because

he had not been made Pope, and who had split in consequence
Christendom in twain. If one splits other men, one will oneself
be split; and so in the bolgia of the schismatics Mahomet is slashed
down from head to middle, almost in two, and all his entrails
hang about his thighs. And Dante, who had looked with a
registering eye upon the pusillanimous, does not falter as he gazes
on Mahomet.

> Già veggia, per mezzul perdere o lulla,
> com'io vidi un, cosí non si pertugia,
> rotto dal mento infin dove si trulla:
>   tra le gambe pendevan le minugia:
> la corata pareva e'l triste sacco
> che merda fa di quel che si trangugia.   (*Inf.* XXVIII, 22–7)

It is the details of this repulsive scene which Dante is anxious to
press home upon our senses. Nor is it wrong, since it is for Dante
the manifestation of divine justice on one who has offended it.
It is Mahomet who is wrong, his treatment which is right. We
are no longer looking from a distance, in order to magnify.
We are looking close at hand, in order to stigmatize. Nor is
there any place for pity in our looking. For the wounds of
Deiphobus were wrong and hurtful, and we may shed our tears
over them. The wounds of Mahomet are right, they are part of
our beatitude, or of our punishment. We may exult in them if
we have escaped them, and by full comprehension of them we
shall tremble the more salutarily if we are in danger of them.
Hell and damnation are good, though not for the damned. They
are the necessary manifestation of divine justice, which would be
left inarticulate without them. It cannot be Boileau's formula,

> Ce qu' on ne doit point voir, qu' un récit nous l'expose,

because Dante has no other mission than to see, and to record,
so that we may see also.

Shall we not gain, thinks Dante, from realizing graphically the
dangers that attend upon our actions? And that being so is something which makes his language at this point supremely un-
Virgilian; so much so, and so typically so, that I find no sense
left in Mr. Eliot's discussion of a *common style* as the characteristic
of a classic. 'In modern European literature, the closest approx-
imation to the ideal of a common style, is probably to be found in
Dante and in Racine; the nearest we have to it in English poetry

is Pope, and Pope's is a common style which, in comparison, is of a very narrow range.' Surely, the juxtaposition of Dante along-side either Pope or Racine cannot be other than a misleading one? Whatever may have been the advance in his views on style and language after he broke off the *De Vulgari Eloquentia*, Dante still maintains a distinction between his *comedy* (which represents a lowliness of style) and Virgil's *tragedy* (which represents a height). Virgil's is the *style noble*, and he has no use for the *mot bas*, plebeian or colloquial, which comes so pungently, and so necessarily, to Dante. Let us take one of the grand Virgilian lines, and I hope, a typical one:

> Et nunc magna mei sub terras ibit imago.
> Urbem praeclaram statui, mea moenia vidi.   (IV, 654–5)

Not a word there need be above the tone of ordinary discourse. But the line?—it is firm and full with the value of human activity. And perhaps we should already contrast it with the episode of St. Francis in *Paradiso* XI to take full measure of the difference between the two poets. At least, it shows us that it is the *idée noble* (the substance underlying the form) which is the essence of the style. Virgil's line is a conflation, something that builds up to a façade. Dante's is supple and plastic, working in reverse towards the identification of an object. It is this difference which excludes from Virgil the trivial or vulgar particular which is essential to Dante; and which is characteristic of Dante's use even where it might not at first sight seem to be essential (*si ch'è la muffa dov'era la gromma*). We see now the significance of the barrel-bottom, gaping wide. Try to insert it in the *Aeneid*, or in the *récit de Théramène* at the end of *Phèdre*, neither Racine nor Virgil would thank you for it. It is too squalid, too trivial, and too graphic. But what is in its essence more squalid than hell, or than the baseness of mankind which feeds it? And the triviality, is not that essential too? It is not everyone who has, like Dante, the privilege of a pre-view. And therefore Dante is all the time seeking the particular which will give graphic em-phasis to what should strike our eyes, or strike our ears. Instead of the noble uniformity which the style of Virgil or of Racine gives to things and people which are disparate, we have in the *Inferno* the constant tendency to diversity. We may not have seen Mahomet walking round with such a hole all down his middle; but we may know how beer-barrels are made, and how the daylight will come through them when the bottom falls apart. This is of the same order as the celebrated image a few cantos earlier by which Dante sharpens our perception of the interchange between man and snake, a metamorphosis we may have never seen: but burn paper, and over its whiteness a new brown tint will creep![1] So here one creature merging horribly into a different one. What employment would Virgil find for such an image?

It will be remembered that Mr. Eliot has, and rightly, pointed out the strict utility of these minor images in Dante: his voyage through the supernatural world would seem nebulous, were it not tied down to things which are most concrete for us, and most visible. It is to be added that this makes for an illusion of clarity, rather than for clarity itself; and this will explain well enough the undistinguished tradition of illustration to Dante's poem. It is the thing we know we visualize clearly, not the other for which it has been substituted: the paper burning, not the metamorphosis in progress of man into snake. And a picture of paper burning, its white turning brown, if easy is not interesting, any more than one of the three pieces, straight and curved, that make up a barrel bottom. On the other side, no precision of image in his parts can make Geryon easy to depict in his whole. But the use of simile is thus a functional opposite in Virgil and in Dante. For Virgil, it is an overtone, something that emphasizes the importance of an incident, colours and magnifies it, and in so doing needs to be important or attractive in itself. In Dante, it is an undertone, something that brings the strange and visionary down to the level of the familiar. It has therefore no obligation whatsoever to be attractive, or even nice. It may sort instead with the terrible description of the adulators' lot, plunged in human excrement,[2] where the dantesque note is also the non-virgilian. But even if it is free from their embarrassments, the dantesque image will tend to be non-pictorial by nature, its duty being to annotate and explain, instead of to flood with light and atmosphere. Thus we have seen it in the bolgia of the simoniacs: 'And as a flame on greasy things moves only on the outer husk, so was it there from heel to tip of toe.' And as an instance of the necessity of this poetic method in the *Comedy* I may quote the scene in the wood of the suicides. They also

[1] *Inf.* XXV, 64-6.   [2] *Inf.* XVIII, 103-17.

suffer the *contrappasso*. They broke the prison of the body, and are in a viler case that will not be broken. They fled the trials of the world, and are exposed to all the haps of this evil wood. They thought to destroy their faculties, and it is the lowest one—the vegetative—which remains eternal, while the sensitive faculty only responds to the stimulus of the pain they fled. Dante comes into this wood of bare and twisted trees. How should he know, or Virgil make him understand, that each tree holds within its bark an imprisoned suicide? Hence the twig plucked, and the tree's protest, and Dante's speaking with Piero della Vigna. But will Dante's testimony be enough for us? And how shall we envisage the problem of talking with twig-ends? Dante feels the obvious need to pass the object-lesson on to us, for fear we should be sceptical. He invents the simile of the green twig burning at one end, and at the other, bubbling and hissing with escaping sap. And he gives to his verse the sound as well as the sense,

> e cigola come vento che va via.

That is the phenomenon, not the emotion about the phenomenon, and no poet bends and breaks his line to onomatopoeia as often, or as successfully, as Dante in this effort to seize all the sense impressions of his voyage, and transfer them unimpaired to us. This is still true, I think, with some of the affectionate images of the *Paradiso*, where Dante wishes to convey at the same time the atmosphere of intimate relationship: as with St. Peter and St. James, whose meeting is concretized as that of doves billing and cooing,[1] or with the contemplative spirits, who turn back up to Mary like a baby at the breast turning with a smile to its mother after its feed.[2] Without the simile we might be uncertain of seeing anything; but with it we are seeing something other than what we started with, and something that is perhaps inadequate as a substitute. It is in the nature of a *trompe l'oeil*. We look up into the church's dome, and seem to see clouds and celestial inhabitants, but what we really see is only paint and perspective. And such similes are explanatory without being visual and certainly without being pictorial. They seem complete because they replace instead of expanding the image from which they start. And this replacement is not normally observed, because the image is not really a simile (i.e. something like what Dante saw), but the essence of

[1] *Par.* XXV, 18–20.　　　[2] *Par.* XXIII, 121–2.

what he sees. The dantesque simile is in the main something
which establishes identity, not something which enhances it; its
function is to inform, not to enthuse. That is, I think, a counter
to the classic use of simile. It is not the procedure of descant and
magnification by association with other ideas which expand and
amplify the first. It is not the familiar which is exalted by comparison, and suffused with the warmth and colour of the poet's
admiration; it is the unfamiliar which is made homely, the unreal
which is given shape and place for us. And we must notice too,
while we are about it, to avoid as well the charge of generalizing
from Dante's necessary practice in the *Inferno*, that the trick of
style by which Dante, in opposition to Virgil, uses humble objects
to explain himself lasts until the very climax of his poem. At
the supreme moment St. Bernard sees the need to cut things short
to suit Dante's mortality, and turns from mystic contemplation
of the innermost mysteries to act *as a good tailor, who cuts his coat
according to the length of stuff he has.*[1] And we may, perhaps, in
this whole matter, take as significant of a divergence in tendency
the recurrence of a motif, almost a signature-tune, in the two
poets. In Virgil it is the note

> Par levibus ventis volucrique simillima somno,
> > > (II, 794; VI, 702)

often repeated in several guises, and essentially a spiritualization
of matter. In Dante it is an opposite rhythm, though again often
repeated, but which, for obvious reasons, I quote from the
Purgatorio and the *Paradiso*,

> come per l'acqua il pesce andando al fondo . . .
> > > (*Purg.* XXVI, 135)
> come per acqua cupa cosa grave . . .   (*Par.* III, 123)

As through dark water sinks some heavy thing: it is a materialization
of what was spiritual. Virgil's line had an ascending rhythm by
which weight and substance vanish into air; Dante's descends
with a gathering of gravity, bringing weight and substance with
it. It is the symbol of the fact that Dante in a way must always
make the mistake of Statius, 'treating the shadows as a solid
thing,'

> trattando l'ombre come cosa salda.   (*Purg.* XXI, 136)

[1] *Par.* XXXII, 139–41.

That care for particularization extends far with Dante. Farinata is the first who remarks to him 'Thy speech bewrayeth thee.' And, indeed, Dante had placed three Tuscanisms in the words which Farinata overheard, wrung from Dante in a moment of personal embarrassment. But this means of identification he uses constantly in the *Inferno*. Pier della Vigna speaks the language of the Chanceries, with its involved solemnity of utterance. Others give away their Bolognese or Lucchese origin by dialectal traits. All are diversified in speech. That is, I think, a contrast with the *Aeneid*. One might read the latter through more than once, and never realize that words were put into different mouths. It is Virgil who speaks, and in his celebration imposes on all the noble uniformity of his style. That is something which is his, and of his time, and not of that of his characters. 'On n'avait alors nulle idée,' said Taine of Livy, 'de la grossièreté antique.' And was it not Taine who first complained of those primitive Romans, who speak all of them in Livy's pages as if they had the oratory of Cicero at their command? That is probably a cogent criticism against a historian; but we should not care to use it against Virgil, however much truth there might be in it. And in a way, if we look for it we can find enough of the 'grossièreté antique' in the *Aeneid* to satisfy ourselves that we do not live in the world of Virgil's heroes, even though we might wish to live in the world of Virgil's poetry. The blood of many bulls offered in sacrifice, the entrails freshly roasted over the camp-fire, the slaves' throats cut by Aeneas (*pius Aeneas*) as a sacrifice, what have we in common with all this? If we read the account in Book V of the games in honour of Anchises' memory we cannot but feel that the cestus match with its brutal battering, with Dares carried senseless and bleeding from the field, coughing up his teeth, and Entellus who remains to display his prowess by felling the bull instead of Dares, is not a form of entertainment we should care to attend in commemoration of our dead relatives. All this—and it forms the counterpart of those windows onto the primitive past which Taine wished more frequent in Livy's history—represents the raw material of Virgil's poem. But it is, of course, with the reverse of a historical interest that we approach poetry; at least, Virgilian poetry. We are not concerned with the archaic, but with the progression from it; and, once more, we may read the *Aeneid* several times before we string together

these material circumstances as one sort of web to the poem.
That is because they are by no means the substance of the poem.
They are neither what is wrong nor what is right: they are what
has been superseded. They are the foundations, and not the house.
But by virtue of the different formula which we have seen
belongs to Dante, how much they would have been seared upon
our vision could they, by some stretch of the imagination, have
entered into the world of the *Comedy*!

Instead, they are for Virgil a residue. He is, of course, very far
from having a Homeric appetite, even in the details which he
takes over, and which he attenuates in taking over. Aeneas cuts
the slaves' throats, but how slight an emphasis is there on this
compared with the episode of Achilles and the young and noble
Trojans whom he sacrifices with the horses and the dogs to
Patroclus. There, there is the smell and taste of blood. The spirit
of the *Iliad* is consonant with Achilles' rejection of Hector's
plea for pity to whichever corpse: 'No pact between man and
lion, no peace to break the eternal war of lamb and wolf; and
between us two neither oath nor any friendship till one of us shall
fall and sate unconquered Mars with blood.' The *Iliad* is full of
exultation in the clash of arms and in the tearing down of what
had been built up, or had seemed fair and strong. But not for
nothing does Virgil claim his descent from Hector and the
Trojans, not from the Greeks. The spirit of the *Aeneid* is the
reverse of the *Iliad*:

> bella horrida bella . . .   (VI, 86)
> Arma amens capio nec sat rationis in armis . . .   (II, 314)

Instead of Agamemnon's prayer for the pleasure of seeing the
hostile flame licking the palace-walls of Troy, with Hector's
breastplate pierced and all his friends biting the dust around him,
we have in Virgil the pathos of Ilium's fall. 'The ancient city
crashes, having ruled for many years,'

> Urbs antiqua ruit multos dominata per annos.   (II, 363)

It is the waste, and not the thrill, which stirs Virgil. Oddly,
because of this, it has seemed to many that the note of Virgil's
poem is one of frustration, that he is essentially doubting and
sceptical, his quiddity the 'lacrimae rerum.' But this interpretation of Virgil's uneasiness, though it has great sanction, does not
quite register. Virgil takes over the poetic material of Homer,

the combat-epic, but his attitude, and the purpose of his poem, is one that has already superseded it. The difficulty of the *Aeneid* is that the second half can not fulfil the promise of the first. The key theme of the opening *Aeneid* can be found by following the one word *moenia*—the city walls—in its periodical recurrences. It is the building of the fabric of civilization that Virgil is concerned with, and the conclusion of it all (which is nothing doubtful) is that

> longa est iniuria, longae
> Ambages; sed summa sequar fastigia rerum.   (I, 341–2)

The travail of the way is long, but we go forward to the heights: that is, of course, to the achievement of Augustus. All this demands a climax, and equally it cannot receive it, except as hints and prophecies, in the latter half of the *Aeneid*, since it so plainly exceeds the theme of Aeneas himself. What we have in lieu of climax is the set of obstacles which attend the beginning of the process; and no effort of the imagination can identify the mere defeat of Turnus with the Roman *summa fastigia rerum*. This is enough to explain the diffidence of Virgil, his feeling at the end that another poem would be more right, his wish to cancel what he had written, and his inability to give completion. The misfortune of the *Aeneid* is that it ought to emerge from the Homeric epic to be something quite different, and yet it finds itself falling backwards in its close instead of moving forwards. Instead of rising in a crescendo the second half can only dwindle. That is disturbing, to the poet, and to his reader; and to this artistic difficulty people have added their evaluation of Virgil's 'philosophy,' which is surely superficial and perfunctory, an adjunct or an ornament, rather than something substantial or vital in itself. What evidence is there for Buxton's view of Book VI, with its descent to Hades, as being the central (as distinct from the middle) part of the *Aeneid*, except in so far as it sets the seal of prophecy on the destiny of Rome? It is this last which matters, not the incidental remarks on metempsychosis or on the ordering of the hereafter. After all, you cannot go down to Hades to learn of your own greatness and see nothing there. But it is by preoccupation with these other matters that men have been able to concentrate on the element of doubt in Virgil's mind, to the exclusion of that of certainty. But the latter is not lacking, and certainly is not intended to be inoperative. The *Iliad*

G

was the poem of war, and of would-be war: the *Aeneid* is the poem of wars, and of would-be peace. That represents another formula, one that looks forward from eternal war to its cessation: 'Then war shall cease, and the rough age grow mild,'

> Aspera tum positis mitescent saecula bellis.   (I, 291)

This is the conviction of Virgil, not that of Homer; and what will be our interest if it should be fulfilled? We shall build our city.

> Miratur molem Aeneas magalia quondam,
> Miratur portas strepitumque et strata viarum.   (I, 421–2)

What is Aeneas's reaction to this spectacle?—'Blessed are they whose walls already rise!'

> O fortunatos! quorum jam moenia surgunt.   (I, 437)

Is it not what he is waiting to see for himself? Virgil is the poet of civilization, not of war, and it is in this operation of the rising walls that all his satisfaction finds expression, not in the crash with which they fall, or in the bonfire with which the palace burns.

> Jura dabat legesque viris operumque laborem
> Partibus aequabat justis aut sorte trahebat.   (I, 508–9)

Is this only Dido at work? What matter if it is, since it holds writ for us as well? 'The city that I build is yours,'

> Urbem quam statuo vestra est.   (I, 573)

If any five words could stand for the essence of Virgil, these they would be. Here there is neither doubting nor frustration. The city is not Carthage only, it is Rome as well; and out of this same process will come the transformation of the Capitol, bristling once with bushes, golden now with palaces,

> Hinc ad Tarpeiam sedem et Capitolia ducit,
> Aurea nunc, olim silvestribus horrida dumis;   (VIII, 347–8)

but it will still expand after that, until the whole world knows its benefit, and Rome gives law and order to the world,

> ac totum sub leges mitteret orbem.   (IV, 231)

Have we lost sight of Dante in this attempt to establish the central concern of Virgil? If we have, it is because Dante is still

going on a divergent course. For him the Capitol is hispid now,
and the gold is in the remotest past: is not that the specific theme
of the colossus of Crete in *Inferno* XIV? The world is no longer,
as it should be, under those laws, and the prosperity it knows in
patches is therefore wrong and injurious. The milk of Virgil's
contentment has turned to gall. Instead of satisfaction we have
the mocking irony of *Inferno* XXVI: 'Florence, rejoice, since
you are grown so great you flap your wings by land and sea, and
spread your name abroad in Hell!'

> Godi, Fiorenza, poi che se' sí grande,
> che per mare e terra batti l'ali,
> e per lo Inferno il tuo nome si spande!   (*Inf.* XXVI, 1–3)

That is Dante, and could not be Virgil; and it is flanked by the
famous invective of ten cantos earlier: ' "Upstarts and sudden
profits have produced, Florence, in you such overweening
pride, that you already weep for it!" '

> "La gente nuova e i subiti guadagni
> orgoglio e dismisura han generata,
> Fiorenza, in te, sí che tu già ten piagni!"   (*Inf.* XVI, 73–5)

While both of these are reinforced by the specific rejection of
the gold of Florence in *Paradiso* IX: ' "Your town ... produces
and it spreads abroad the cursed flower[1] which sends the sheep and
lambs astray, for it has turned the shepherd to a wolf." ' This goes
even further than a lamentation for the absence of the Emperor
to order the world aright: it expresses a distrust for the substance
of prosperity itself. It is obviously something quite distinct from
Virgil's pride in the golden Capitol. And we can carry the opposition further, and make it even more formal and precise. Virgil's
satisfaction overflows, quite naturally, onto the proper names
that form the Roman scene of action:

> qui nunc Misenus ab illo
> Dicitur, aeternumque tenet per saecula nomen.
> (VI, 234–5)

That is a full statement, one which leaves no room for any
Virgilian tremor. Surely, the *lacrimae rerum* are for the things
which are sad, and the tone here is one of exultation and achievement? And look how it leads away from Dante. Dante has a

---

[1] I.e., the lily, standing for the Florentine gold florin.

famous account of the River Arno, with a damning catalogue of those who live beside its banks. It was the river of Florence, the Florence of Dante's birth, and of the *bel san Giovanni*, but nonetheless it is

> la maladetta e sventurata fossa,   (*Purg.* XIV, 51)

the damned and wretched ditch. Had doubting Virgil any tears to shed, or better, had he any wrath to pour, over the Roman Tiber? But no, it is instead

> caelo gratissimus amnis,

the river most pleasing to the gods. Dante has no praise, but only scorn and condemnation, for his world of 1300, because it is going wrong. But Virgil's world is going right. Man is no longer the plaything of the gods (they kill us for their sport), as he was for Homer:

> Numina nulla premunt; mortali urgemur ab hoste
> Mortales.   (X, 375)

The rôle of the gods has changed: they swell the actors, instead of breaking up capriciously the action. It is, as we have seen, the Racinian formula:

> Maior agit deus atque opera ad maiora remittit . . .
>   (XII, 429)
> C'est Vénus tout entière à sa proie attachée . . .

Man, in the irreparable briefness of mortal life, can find space for durable accomplishment, and he no longer lives by spoil. The answer of Virgil to the older zest for war and plunder is constant, and decisive. Against the ancient habits of mankind,

> Armati terram exercent semperque recentis
> Convectare juvat praedas et vivere rapto   (VII, 748–9)

we now object with a new affirmation:

> Nulla salus bello; pacem te poscimus omnes.   (XI, 362)

'In war is no salvation: it is peace we all demand of you.' But that is not to initiate inertia, or to make a renunciation of activity. Time hurries us away, but we can bid defiance: 'For each there

stands his day; short and irreparable is the time of life for all; but
to extend one's fame by deeds, that is the task for worth. . . .'

> Stat sua cuique dies; breve et inreparabile tempus
> Omnibus est vitae; set famam extendere factis,
> Hoc virtutis opus. (X, 467–9)

And because that is concerned with our possibilities here, and
remains agnostic as to our possibilities hereafter, it is bound to be
different from anything Dante will put forward. The difference
is a simple one, but it is very far-reaching. Virgil is looking
forward to what one may do: it will be a construction, something, like his poem, which does not exist until it does exist;
something like order invented out of chaos, and then transcending
it. For Dante it is not a question of any new achievements to be
made: neither he nor any other is to cast the bronze, nor is
Florence to be congratulated, except sarcastically, on her achievement of wealth. But there is an order in which everything once
was (or should have been), and was (or would have been) right;
and if only we could accept the right authorities and return, then
everything would again be right. Now, in these circumstances,
it is only an accident that Virgil himself figures on the list of
Dante's authorities, as the singer of the Empire: because the
direction in which the two are going is opposite. For Virgil,
there was something wrong in the past, and Rome has trans-
cended it: for Dante, there is something wrong in the present,
and Italy (or mankind) should abandon it. The *virtutis opus* has
shifted absolutely its ground, and Dante, in consequence, becomes
incoherent in the matter of fame. His temperament acknowledges
the *gran disio dell'eccellenza*, but alongside the statements, and they
are few, which support it there comes a new, and often-repeated,
note: 'What is the rumour of the world but wind, that blows
now here, now there, and changes name because it changes side?
. . . Your reputation is the colour of the grass, which comes and
goes, and he discolours it who brings it freshly from the ground.'

> Blowne in the Morning, thou shalt fade ere Noone:
> What bootes a Life which in such haste forsakes thee?
> Th'art wondrous frolick being to dye so soone:
> And passing proud a little colour makes thee.

> If thee thy brittle beauty so deceives,
> Know then the thing that swells thee is thy bane;
> For the same beauty doth in bloody leaves
> The sentence of thy early death containe.

The time is brief, but it is irreparable only if we use it for its own sake, or outside the plan; and there are no monuments out-lasting brass.

In such conditions, and without our realizing it, attention slips naturally from the details of the world as it should have been organized, so that the right ordering of the active life, though it is postulated, yet it is never envisaged by Dante in more than its externals. Obviously, God had a plan for the world, and the Empire unlocks the door to it. The thing to do is to find the key and go back. If one has lost the key to one's front door one does not set about the building of a house out in the coldness of the elements, one goes down on hands and knees to find the missing key. And precisely because one can go back to a right order there is no call for an explanation of order, or of the steps towards achieving it. One waits for Henry VII to appear; and if he disappears without establishing it, then he was not the DUX, and one must wait again for the true DUX to come. That is why Machiavelli (or Petrarch) is politically more mature than Dante. For, stated thus, civilization is not an achievement, but a restoration. It is behind us, not in front. It cannot be added to, nor embroidered on, since it is an arrangement, not an achievement. The world, for Dante, and hence the constancy of his invective for it from the beginning to the end of the *Commedia*, is as bemerded as are the adulators of the second bolgia. What it needs is ablution, not adornment or building operations. Look at any point for any conception of a positive addition to the texture of civilization in the *Divine Comedy*, and you will find how strikingly the sense of any is absent. But that is quite logical. Indeed, with such a system of ideas, what room could there be for Virgil's postulate,

> Longa est iniuria longae
> Ambages set summa sequar fastigia rerum?

With Dante we are not going forward to a height, we are going backward to our place.

It remains for Dante to deny the elements over which the

order was to have been achieved, and so to deny as well the value
of that place. And this he actually does, and we have seen him
doing it. Indeed, it is one of the most curious parts in M. Gilson's
valuable account of Dante, the one where he announces Dante,
in spite of his theories, as turning out traditional in the matter of
the superiority of the contemplative over the active life. As if it
left the theories undisturbed! Dante was within an ace of
establishing a double beatitude for man; he was ready to assert
the primacy of what was within our reach, because it was best,
not perhaps in itself, but at least *pour nous*. And then he turned his
back upon his own creation. It is the sidestep of the middle of the
Purgatorio. The child likes the apple: it is, says Dante, a natural
childish appetite, and so it should be, it must be, right and
satisfactory, because instinctive love can not go wrong,

> Lo natural è sempre sanza errore.   (*Purg.* XVII, 94)

By that sanction we might at least avoid the discomfort of scout-
ing fur in Russia (what's its use in France?), and have Dante's
approval for our contentment with the stage at which we are.
But right from the start this theory of natural love is inhibited
by a disturbing note: ' "The new and simple soul knows nothing
. . . feels the lure at first of little goods; here is deceived," '

> "L'anima semplicetta che sa nulla . . .
> . . . Di picciol bene in pria sente sapore;
> quivi s'inganna."   (*Purg.* XVI, 88; 91–2)

Surely, by virtue of Dante's theory, what was little had the right
to like what was little, and is good, without a question of its
being deceived thereby? Perhaps the apple (like Eve's) is not so
natural, or being natural, is not so right, as it appeared to be?
' "So let us say that every love rises within you by necessity, but
it is in your power to keep it there," '

> "Onde pognam che di necessitate
> surga ogni amor che dentro a voi s'accende,
> di ritenerlo è in voi la podestate."   (*Purg.* XVIII, 70–2)

By this we may be condemned to like the apple, but we must
hesitate as to whether we shall do well to proceed to eat it up.
Nor can we say that reason's task is but to stop us from the
consumption of too many apples, for Dante's next step, and this
no further off than in his next canto, is to sum the matter up with

the dream of the *femmina balba*. Here the natural love is no longer *sanza errore*. It is the opposite of this, since it is in itself full of corruptions, and it is only our twisting view of it that perverts it into something attractive or appetising. The apple (and let it symbolize the *false* attractions of this world) was really rotten within, and reason when we hesitated should have told us so. From heaven there comes a holy lady to unmask the siren whose sweet singing has perverted Dante's taste: 'She took the other one, and opened her in front, rending her clothes to let her belly show; and that awaked me with the stench which it gave out,'

> L'altra prendeva, e dinanzi l'apria,
> fendendo i drappi, e mostravami il ventre:
> quel mi svegliò col puzzo che n'uscia.   (*Purg.* XIX, 31–3)

This has gone further than the ablution which was to wash the world clean: what is now posited is one to wash it all away. And Dante, when he wakes up, runs the risk of having nothing to wake up to. But, of course, he is able to avoid a vacuum because he replaces the attempt to sanctify the natural—which plainly after such language cannot still be done—by the acceptance of the supernatural. The *Inferno* is the world that is wrong; but the *Purgatorio* does not turn out to be the world that is being put right (as it both should, and should not, be). It is instead the call to the abandonment of the world. ' "Heaven as it revolves about you calls to you and shows you its eternal beauty, and yet your eye looks only to the earth!" '

> "Chiamavi il cielo e'ntorno vi si gira,
> mostrandovi le sue bellezze eterne,
> e l 'occhio vostro pur a terra mira!" (*Purg.* XIV, 148–50)

In the wrongness of the world it is now not the stimulus or the direction to go right—that is, away—which is lacking: it is the muzzle that held here to order, and which completes this passage of *Purgatorio*. " 'That was the harsh curb which should keep man within his bounds,' "

> "Quel fu il duro camo
> che dovria l'uom tener dentro a sua meta."
>
> (*Purg.* XIV, 143–4)

If it were to do so, it would effectually prevent him from

attaining to the *summa fastigia rerum*; but by Dante's confession
to Beatrice man had no rightful function within that bound. It
is a lesson painfully learnt, and one that moves Dante to tears.
But it is one which sticks, and which supplants the earlier ones.
And so we have seen it already: 'Weeping I said: "Scarcely was
your face hidden from me than present things with their false
pleasure turned my steps." '[1] What should we do but abandon
the present for the eternal? Dante's poem is a pencil sharpened
to the clearest of points, with which he writes a blank cheque on
a theoretic slate for the universal monarchy of Pope and
Emperor. But the pencil point is broken for us now. In between
there has come Machiavelli with his repudiation of sovereignty
and his resolute affirmation that 'any absolute authority corrupts
the matter in the shortest time, making itself friends and parti-
sans.' It could not then unite, as Dante thought, but only corrupt
and divide. The pencil point is broken, the slate not there to
write on. We have neither Dante now to dream of universal
monarchy, nor Harrington to dream of universal righteous
empire. But what matter? The pencil point was broken for
Dante too: only, it was sharpened also at the other end. But will
not its point be therefore in the air? Precisely, it is our pointer
upwards from the unordered world. Indeed, the right ordering
of human activity, defined by Aristotle, and controlled by the
Emperor, was so much a hypothesis that Dante never manages
to state its scope himself, he even comes resolutely to its exclusion.
Gentile saw in Dante's political views the revolt against medieval
transcendentalism; and M. Gilson counselled caution. *En effet*, if
the Emperor only escapes from the jurisdiction of the Pope
because he stands immediately under that of God the process
hardly involves any autonomy of a new lay state. And in
practice (which Dante did not get as far as considering) it might
be a little difficult to disentangle things which are to be both
identical and wholly separate. But Dante's final utterances dismiss
the hypothesis of the active life by reaccepting the contemplative
ideal as a superior one. Is not human activity a diversion from
man's proper concern, which is not himself, but God? ' "To this
little star there are assigned good spirits who were active so that
fame and honour might ensue to them; and when desires rest on

[1] *Purg.* XXXI, 34–6.

this, going only wrong in this, then must the rays of true love rest less brightly up above." '

> "Questa picciola stella si correda
> de'buoni spiriti che son stati attivi,
> perché onore e fama li succeda:
>   e quando li disiri poggian quivi,
> sí disviando, pur convien che i raggi
> del vero amore in su poggin men vivi."   (*Par.* VI, 112–7)

For, viewed from one angle, activity *here* is inactivity *there*. Dante is thus a little like our educationalists, who cry out that it is most essential for every child to have two more years at school, and then omit to explain what they propose the child should learn within that period. Without announcing or justifying the change that has taken place in his views Dante turns aside from the thought of organization, so easily left out of the *De Monarchia*, and direction (for human activity can hardly be only the squirrel on the revolving wheel), and renounces the world. His operative ideal is St. Francis, not Augustus; and not St. Francis alongside Augustus; and we can only take the declarations of *Paradiso* XXII as representing a definitive alignment which places Dante in the medieval tradition, when it had seemed before from some of his hypotheses that he might be ready to sanction the Renascence. As he looks down from Paradise we saw how he smiled at the poor (and needless) show the world makes,

> tal ch'io sorrisi del suo vil sembiante;
>   e quel consiglio per migliore approbo
> che l'ha per meno; e chi ad altro pensa
> chiamar si puote veramente probo.   (*Par.* XXII, 135–8)

'And he who thinks of other things can truly be called just.' What is this world, *en fin de compte*? Only 'the little patch of earth that makes us all so fierce,'

> L'aiuola che ci fa tanto feroci.   (*ibid.* 151)

What should we do about it? We should turn away:

> Poscia rivolsi gli occhî agli occhî belli.   (*ibid.* 154)

In Virgil there is the golden Capitol, the city founded, the bustle of the streets, and the rising of the walls. For Dante, these are *senseless cares*, and we shall do better to strip ourselves of them.

' "Oh unknown riches, fruitful good! Aegidius casts his shoes away, Sylvester does so too, following the bridegroom, so pleasing was the bride," '

> "Oh ignota ricchezza, oh ben ferace!
> Scalzasi Egidio, scalzasi Silvestro
> dietro allo sposo; sí la sposa piace."   (*Par.* XI, 82–4)

St. Francis's bride was Poverty, and Dante ends by detemporalizing not only the Church, but man as well, in spite of his beginnings. 'Le bonheur temporel de l'individu par la sagesse humaine, voilà donc la leçon qu'enseigne le *Banquet*. Le salut temporel de l'humanité par l'Empire, telle sera la conclusion de la *Monarchie*. Le salut éternel des hommes par l'Eglise, ce sera l'enseignement ultime de la *Divine Comédie*.' M. Gilson's formula seems very neat and equitable: but how can it work if the last item pre-empts the other two? if we should do well to take the *enseignement ultime* first, to the exclusion of all else? But Dante does not turn back to decide compatibilities. And in the meantime, if for him the ideal of Poverty represents unknown riches, and happy are they who shed their shoes and follow it, Virgil is explicitly loth to keep him company. Before the vestibule of Dis, in the very jaws of death, with pale disease, old age, fear and evil-counselling hunger, there lives foul poverty,

> Pallentesque habitant morbi tristisque senectus
> Et metus et malesuada fames ac turpis egestas,
> Terribiles visu formae . . .   (VI, 275–7)

forms terrible to look upon: *so pleasing was the bride*;

> "poscia di dí in dí l'amò piú forte,"   (*Par.* XI, 61)

turpis egestas. Is there a link between the world of St. Francis and that of Virgil?

We must add, too, that Dante never had so far to travel to reach the ideal of St. Francis. The condemnation of riches as the cheapest trash (*vilissime cose*) is of the *Convivio*; the idea of Fortune as no longer the blind goddess of the ancients, but as the blind instrument of Providence instead, is of the *De Monarchia*, and is enshrined at the beginning of the *Inferno*. ' "Master," said to him, "now tell me this as well: this Fortune, whom you touch upon, what is she, to have within her clutches so the wealth of all the world?" '

> "Maestro" diss'io lui, "or mi di'anche:
> questa Fortuna, di che tu mi tocche,
> che è, che i ben del mondo ha sí tra branche?"
>
> (*Inf.* VII, 67–9)

In her clutches is the empty treasure of the world's wealth: it is not something which man has achieved, or added to a primitive existence. It is something outside his control, beyond defence of human wits,

> oltre la difension de'senni umani, (*ibid.* 81)

and before it, like the order of the world. It is, if we like, the negation of Virgil's affirmative:

> Urbem quam statuo *non* vestra est;

and the whole purpose of Fortune's rôle is to ensure that man should attach no importance to the goods which *she* dispenses: ' "Now can you see, my son, how short the jest is of the goods committed into Fortune's care, for which the human race makes strife," '

> "Or puoi, figliuol, veder la corta buffa
> de'ben che son commessi alla Fortuna,
> per che l'umana gente si rabbuffa . . ." (*ibid.* 61–3)

Once more, did Dante's enthusiasm for Virgil strike the prelude for the Renascence? We can see at a glance how little preparation there is here for ideas which are essential to that movement. Leon Battista Alberti also will distrust *wealth*, but because he sees something by the side of it which can be built up also, and is preferable: 'I hate sumptuosity, and I delight in those things which are the invention of the mind and are graceful and pleasurable.'[1] We are no longer there on the old ground where wealth was a capricious issue from Fortune, and the new distrust arises from the emergence of a different (and a constructive concept,) which is Taste, or discretion. With wealth, or without it, we may add something which was not there before, and which is there because we made it. It is the voice of Raphael, looking for the principle of beauty, as something to create. Was Raphael in

---

[1] Cf. Whitfield, *Petrarch and the Renascence*, 164.

Fortune's clutches, as a predetermined lucky dip? or is he the fabric
of civilization, something which we have inherited, wealth or no
wealth, because of his achievement? It is because he left no room
for man to build on that the Renascence dismissed Dante as a
primitive. For Poetry is Dante's art, and alongside it there are
no also-rans; and when, as in the reliefs of *Purgatorio*, he ventures
into the world of visual art it is with other criteria than those of
taste: 'The dead seemed dead, the living seemed alive, and he
who saw the things themselves had seen no better than myself,'

> Morti li morti, e i vivi parean vivi:
> non vide me'di me chi vide il vero;   (*Purg.* XII, 67–8)

the principle of which is television (with depth in time, instead of
only in space), not Taste.

   With Virgil we are on different ground. It is the function of
literature, as exemplified in Virgil's poetry, to create an atmosphere above and around the world of realities, in which the
mental activity of man can then exist and expand; just as his
physical activity has done already in the circumambient belt of air.
It is here that literature makes its tremendous contribution to life,
by this creation of a new plane on which to live. Literature, like
the arts, is a contribution, that is, an addition, to the texture of
life. It is the humus that supports the vegetation above the arid
rock. That is why, in spite of his lines about the warrior-poet,
who

> Semper equos atque arma virum pugnasque canebat—
>   (IX, 775)

which seems intended for himself as well by implication—Virgil
prepares the interests of the gentleman, not of the nobleman: art
and literature, not war and the chase; if we wish to see the picture
down the centuries, not Henry Hastings, but Horace Walpole.
He is concerned with something that builds itself up above the
pattern of life, with the emotions that arise from the pattern,
more than with the pattern itself. It is a concern which adds a
new pattern, a human one replacing a mechanical one. And the
same question we asked about Raphael we may also ask about
Virgil: was the *Aeneid* in Fortune's clutches *ab initio*, waiting to
be dispensed at her dictation? Or should we say something
different? that the bulls, the cestus, the blood-bath, this is what
Virgil has risen over, what we should measure his stature by, as

an advance in civilization? his stature and our gratitude? That
is a humanist formula; and Virgil is the most humanist of poets.
Might we not take as being applicable to Virgil, so interpreted,
the plea of Paracelsus?

> I never fashioned out a fancied good
> Distinct from man's; a service to be done,
> A glory to be ministered unto,
> With powers put forth at man's expense, withdrawn
> From labouring in his behalf, a strength
> Denied that might avail him. I cared not
> Lest his success ran counter to success
> Elsewhere: for God is glorified in man,
> And to man's glory vowed I soul and limb.

Urbem quam statuo vestra est. Remove from Paracelsus's statement
what makes it post-Christian in its detail, and it might be the
utterance of Virgil. Leave it as it is, and it might be the answer
of Virgil-guide to the rôle thrust upon him by Dante in the
Comedy. For this is as clear and unmistakable as their attitudes
to the Tiber and the Arno: with Virgil, we shall make the most of
what is round about us; but with Dante?—we shall make the
least of it. 'With my eyes I then went back through all the seven
spheres, and saw this globe such that I smiled at its puny air; and
for the best I take that counsel which makes the least of it; and he
who thinks of other things can truly be called just.'

> Col viso ritornai per tutte quante
> le sette spere, e vidi questo globo
> tal, ch'io sorrisi del suo vil sembiante;
>   e quel consiglio per migliore approbo
> che l'ha per meno; e chi ad altro pensa
> chiamar si puote veramente probo.   (*Par.* XXII, 133–8)

So Virgil is going towards civilization, and Dante is going
towards Paradise. So two may meet who are going in opposite
directions, and may meet because they are going in opposite
directions, and can come face to face before they leave, each
separately, the other one behind. Their names are indissolubly
linked, both in their magnitude, and in the relationship of Dante
to Virgil-guide. Their poetry, unless I am mistaken, touches only
very slightly. And it is here that the curve of their respective
fortunes is instructive in its contrast. The medieval acquaintance

with Virgil, which Dante inherited, is different from the Renascence one. And the Renascence, we may say, sees Virgil in, and Dante out. From now on Dante and Virgil tend to play the fox and goat of La Fontaine's fable: the one goes up while the other goes down. Europe clings to Virgil as the major poet until the end of the eighteenth century. The nineteenth century sees the wane of Virgil's reputation, and the full swell, after a long hiatus, of Dante's. That does not suggest a feeling in the minds of their readers of the two poets being overmuch alike; it corroborates the impression of their difference. Nor must we take the easy option of saying that Virgil pleased the Renascence just because he was antique. We might more easily say that he displeased the nineteenth century for that reason, and because he was *graceful and imitative* (by logical inference from current theory), while Dante was forceful, primitive, and, therefore, real. But it was not a mere prejudice for a dead tongue that made the new generations of the Renascence rank Virgil as high as Dante had done for theological reasons. It was an instinctive sympathy with the humanistic content of Virgil's poetry which made its language live again: an understanding of this quality of the *Aeneid* as a celebration of what man has done with the elements, good and bad, of the world that he is in. For the point of humanism is not where Signor Toffanin would put it, in the idea that in looking back to Virgil, or Cicero, one was fulfilling God's law: that is the point of origin of humanism, the idea that allowed it to exist without infringing orthodoxy. But its centre is in the feeling that one was moving within the fabric of civilization, which man had made, and might continue. For if Dante's order was imaginary, and had ultimately to be shifted, as we saw, outside time into the pre-history of Eden, the order for which Augustus stood was something that had been in history; and the poetry of Virgil, which reflected pride in that achievement, was something real and human. In such conditions it is no accident that the Renascence in its development is partly imitative, but it is mere stupidity to imagine that its substance is imitation. Antiquity is the humus from which the Renascence springs, not the pattern on which it moulds itself. Whom does Petrarch, or Michelangelo, or Machiavelli, exactly resemble, or reproduce? And Virgil both achieves, and offers the possibility of achievement. It is for this that he remains the figurehead of European poetry as long as the Renascence ideal lasted. When it failed, or was abandoned, then only was it possible to look back beyond it, and rediscover the stature of the forgotten Dante. Nor did the nineteenth century, as we have seen, shirk the labour that was necessary for this reconquest of Dante: rather, it was its very existence that assured the nineteenth-century scholars that they stood on the right track. It flattered their strong appetite for work, while at the same time disarming them as critics or appre-ciators. We now stand outside both those traditions, in perhaps a poorer world than either of them knew. At least thereby we may have one advantage, though dearly bought, over either: that of being able to understand them both in their differing statements. And if we do, we have still one contradiction left, and not the least. Dante, we have seen, abandoned the idea of human achievement for the *contemplatio Dei*: 'O senseless care of mortal men, how far defective are the syllogisms that make you flap your wings below! Some went after law, some read the Aphorisms, some followed priesthood, some rule by force or trickery, some robbery, some civil occupations, some laboured wrapped up in the pleasures of the flesh, some gave themselves to ease, whilst I, *set free from all these things*, with Beatrice was up in heaven so gloriously received.'

> O insensata cura de'mortali,
> quanto son difettivi sillogismi
> quei che ti fanno in basso batter l'ali!
>   Chi dietro a iura, e chi ad aforismi
> sen giva, e chi seguendo sacerdozio,
> e chi regnar per forza o per sofismi,
>   e chi rubare, e chi civil negozio,
> chi, nel diletto della carne involto
> s'affaticava, e chi si dava all'ozio,
>   quando, *da tutte queste cose sciolto*,
> con Beatrice m'era suso in cielo
> cotanto gloriosamente accolto.   (*Par.* XI, 1–12).

That lumping together of the activities, good and bad, is the final denial of human activity and achievement, as having a career and a meaning of its own. But . . . had Dante, then, no achieve-ment? Was the *Divine Comedy*—it is the question we asked about the *Aeneid*, and about Raphael, and might still wish to ask about a hundred others whom we admire—part of the pack which

Fortune shuffled, and shuffles still, to baffle us? Is not the *Divine Comedy* also an addition to the humus, an extension of man's mental atmosphere: something that was not, and is, only because it is, and Dante made it so? It is here that Mr. Eliot's discussion of poetic assent, which occurs appropriately enough in his volume on *Dante*, is relevant to our purpose. We may enjoy the poetry, he said, while suspending belief and disbelief. And so perhaps we may. But, nevertheless, if we do so we have betrayed our author at his most conscious point, because the whole purpose of Dante's poem was to establish, and promote, belief. We cannot separate off these levels of enjoyment (the poetical from the theological) of Dante without creating a humanist Eliot and, *se invito*, a humanist Dante. For we shall be back at Vida's counsel, which I quoted before as being other than that of Dr. Moore, and which I may now quote again as being other than that of Dante:

> Nulla dies tamen interea, tibi nulla abeat nox
> Quin aliquid vatum sacrorum e fontibus almis
> Hauseris, ac dulcem labris admoveris amnem.

For that posits, does it not, not that there are elements in Virgil's system of ideas which may be part of the Logos and confirm Christianity, but that there is nourishment there by which the stature of the mind may grow. Nor does it make much difference that Mr. Eliot may innocently have deceived himself when he put down his theory of poetic assent as a suspension of belief, for it seems possible, at least, that his interest in Dante was a hatching of belief, a confirmation of ideas and tendencies, rather than any suspension of them. And yet the very fact of Mr. Eliot conceiving of it as worth while to suspend belief (or disbelief) implies existence of a layer—which is man's achievement and his history—in which man moves with freedom because it is his own, belonging outside him neither to beast nor God. It is for these reasons that if we begin by accepting Dante, we may risk having to reject Virgil; and we may equally well find ourselves rejecting Dante also. 'Whilst I set free from all these things, with Beatrice was up in heaven so gloriously received.' *Qui Christum scit, satis est si cetera nescit.* And obviously even Dante may be here among the *et cetera.* But if we begin by accepting Virgil, we shall run no final risk of rejecting Dante. They are both entities in the experience of man, funds on which we can call, humus from which we can grow, because we come after them, and did not come before them. Nor is Dante, perhaps, unaware of this, and it is by his temper that he joins hands in Italian poetry with one who was as nihilistic as himself, though in a thoroughly different way. When all is reduced finally to *nulla*, to bitterness and nothingness, and Leopardi himself should be included in that reduction, he yet answers with a heroic affirmation that he is something else, and something more: *Maggior mi sento*. And Dante too may bid us turn our eyes from all the senseless cares of men to soar aloft; but might he not expect us still to cast a recognizing glance upon his poem? We may look back to Dante in the company of the noble poets of antiquity in Canto IV of the *Inferno*: 'And much more honour did they do to me, making me one of their own throng, so that I was the sixth amongst such wisdom.' It is a canto through which there echoes, as a leit-motiv, the word that Statius spoke, the claim of *honour*. Who can doubt that Dante means to share as well in all this honour? 'Honour the most high poet' . . . 'They do me honour, and in that do well.' So there may be no Phèdre or Dido here, but there is instead a Dante, who has heroic and poetic stature in his own right, nor shall we need to reject him, any more than Virgil. As individuals, that is; for it may well be our tragedy to live in an age which cannot adhere to the message of either.